Marx Joyce Abbott Hardy Montaigne Machiavelli Chesterton Cooper Emerson Austen Defoe Melville Haggard Hugo Christie Eliot Grimm Stoker Carroll Molière Wilde Maupassant Byron Schiller Garnett Einstein Fitzgerald Engels Goethe Hawthorne Smith Kafka Cotton Dostoyevsky Hall Baum Kipling Doyle Willis Leslie Dumas Henry Nietzsche Flaubert Turgenev Balzac Stockton Vatsyayana Crane Burroughs Verne Curtis Tocqueville Whitman Gogol Vinci Homer Widger Tolstoy Busch Darwin Thoreau Potter Freud Zola Twain Plato Scott Lawrence Kant Jowett Stevenson Dickens Andersen Burton Hesse Harte London Descartes Cervantes Poe Aristotle Wells Voltaire Hale James Hastings Cooke Bunner Shakespeare Richter Chekhov da Chambers Irving Doré Swift Dante Shaw Wodehouse Benedict Alcott Pushkin Newton tredition®

tredition was established in 2006 by Sandra Latusseck and Soenke Schulz. Based in Hamburg, Germany, tredition offers publishing solutions to authors and publishing houses, combined with worldwide distribution of printed and digital book content. tredition is uniquely positioned to enable authors and publishing houses to create books on their own terms and without conventional manufacturing risks.

For more information please visit: www.tredition.com

TREDITION CLASSICS

This book is part of the TREDITION CLASSICS series. The creators of this series are united by passion for literature and driven by the intention of making all public domain books available in printed format again - worldwide. Most TREDITION CLASSICS titles have been out of print and off the bookstore shelves for decades. At tredition we believe that a great book never goes out of style and that its value is eternal. Several mostly non-profit literature projects provide content to tredition. To support their good work, tredition donates a portion of the proceeds from each sold copy. As a reader of a TREDITION CLASSICS book, you support our mission to save many of the amazing works of world literature from oblivion. See all available books at www.tredition.com.

Project Gutenberg

The content for this book has been graciously provided by Project Gutenberg. Project Gutenberg is a non-profit organization founded by Michael Hart in 1971 at the University of Illinois. The mission of Project Gutenberg is simple: To encourage the creation and distribution of eBooks. Project Gutenberg is the first and largest collection of public domain eBooks.

Robert Louis Stevenson

A record, an estimate, and a memorial

Alexander H. (Alexander Hay) Japp

Imprint

This book is part of TREDITION CLASSICS

Author: Alexander H. (Alexander Hay) Japp
Cover design: Buchgut, Berlin – Germany

Publisher: tredition GmbH, Hamburg - Germany
ISBN: 978-3-8424-3817-0

www.tredition.com
www.tredition.de

The intention of the TREDITION CLASSICS series is to make world literature in the public domain available in printed format. Literary enthusiasts and organizations, such as Project Gutenberg, worldwide have scanned and digitally edited the original texts. tredition has subsequently formatted and redesigned the content into a modern reading layout. Therefore, we cannot guarantee the exact reproduction of the original format of a particular historic edition. Please also note that no modifications have been made to the spelling, therefore it may differ from the orthography used today.

ROBERT LOUIS STEVENSON
a record, an estimate, and a memorial

By ALEXANDER H. JAPP, LL.D., F.R.S.E

author of "thoreau: his life and aims"; "memoir of thomas de quincey"; "de quincey memorials," etc., etc.

WITH HITHERTO UNPUBLISHED LETTERS FROM R. L. STEVENSON IN FACSIMILIE . . .

second edition

NEW YORK
CHARLES SCRIBNER'S SONS
153-157 FIFTH AVENUE
1905

Printed in Great Britain.

Dedicated to
C. A. LICHTENBERG, Esq.
and
Mrs LICHTENBERG,

of villa margherita, treviso,
with most grateful regards,

ALEXANDER H. JAPP.

19*thDecember* 1904.

PREFACE

A few words may here be allowed me to explain one or two points. First, about the facsimile of last page of Preface to *Familiar Studies of Men and Books*. Stevenson was in Davos when the greater portion of that work went through the press. He felt so much the disadvantage of being there in the circumstances (both himself and his wife ill) that he begged me to read the proofs of the Preface for him. This illness has record in the letter from him (pp. 28-29). The printers, of course, had directions to send the copy and proofs of the Preface to me. Hence I am able now to give this facsimile.

With regard to the letter at p. 19, of which facsimile is also given, what Stevenson there meant is not the "three last" of that batch, but the three last sent to me before—though that was an error on his part—he only then sent two chapters, making the "eleven chapters now"—sent to me by post.

Another point on which I might have dwelt and illustrated by many instances is this, that though Stevenson was fond of hob-nobbing with all sorts and conditions of men, this desire of wide contact and intercourse has little show in his novels—the ordinary fibre of commonplace human beings not receiving much celebration from him there; another case in which his private bent and sympathies received little illustration in his novels. But the fact lies implicit in much I have written.

I have to thank many authors for permission to quote extracts I have used.

ALEXANDER H. JAPP.

CONTENTS

CHAPTER I—INTRODUCTION AND FIRST IMPRESSIONS

My little effort to make Thoreau better known in England had one result that I am pleased to think of. It brought me into personal association with R. L. Stevenson, who had written and published in *The Cornhill Magazine* an essay on Thoreau, in whom he had for some time taken an interest. He found in Thoreau not only a rare character for originality, courage, and indefatigable independence, but also a master of style, to whom, on this account, as much as any, he was inclined to play the part of the "sedulous ape," as he had acknowledged doing to many others—a later exercise, perhaps in some ways as fruitful as any that had gone before. A recent poet, having had some seeds of plants sent to him from Northern Scotland to the South, celebrated his setting of them beside those native to the Surrey slope on which he dwelt, with the lines—

> "And when the Northern seeds are growing,
> Another beauty then bestowing,
> We shall be fine, and North to South
> Be giving kisses, mouth to mouth."

So the Thoreau influence on Stevenson was as if a tart American wild-apple had been grafted on an English pippin, and produced a wholly new kind with the flavours of both; and here wild America and England kissed each other mouth to mouth.

The direct result was the essay in *The Cornhill*, but the indirect results were many and less easily assessed, as Stevenson himself, as we shall see, was ever ready to admit. The essay on Thoreau was written in America, which further, perhaps, bears out my point.

One of the authorities, quoted by Mr Hammerton, in *Stevensoniana* says of the circumstances in which he found our author, when he was busily engaged on that bit of work:

> "I have visited him in a lonely lodging in California, it was previous to his happy marriage, and found him submerged in billows of bed-clothes; about him floated the scattered volumes of a complete set of Thoreau; he was preparing an essay on

that worthy, and he looked at the moment like a half-drowned man, yet he was not cast down. His work, an endless task, was better than a straw to him. It was to become his life-preserver and to prolong his years. I feel convinced that without it he must have surrendered long since. I found Stevenson a man of the frailest physique, though most unaccountably tenacious of life; a man whose pen was indefatigable, whose brain was never at rest, who, as far as I am able to judge, looked upon everybody and everything from a supremely intellectual point of view." [1]

We remember the common belief in Yorkshire and other parts that a man could not die so long as he could stand up—a belief on which poor Branwell Brontk was fain to act and to illustrate, but R. L. Stevenson illustrated it, as this writer shows, in a better, calmer, and healthier way, despite his lack of health.

On some little points of fact, however, Stevenson was wrong; and I wrote to the Editor of *The Spectator* a letter, titled, I think, "Thoreau's Pity and Humour," which he inserted. This brought me a private letter from Stevenson, who expressed the wish to see me, and have some talk with me on that and other matters. To this letter I at once replied, directing to 17 Heriot Row, Edinburgh, saying that, as I was soon to be in that City, it might be possible for me to see him there. In reply to this letter Mr Stevenson wrote:

"The Cottage, Castleton of Braemar,
Sunday, August (? *th*), 1881.

"My dear Sir,—I should long ago have written to thank you for your kind and frank letter; but, in my state of health, papers are apt to get mislaid, and your letter has been vainly hunted for until this (Sunday) morning.

"I must first say a word as to not quoting your book by name. It was the consciousness that we disagreed which led me, I daresay, wrongly, to suppress *all* references throughout the paper. But you may be certain a proper reference will now be introduced.

"I regret I shall not be able to see you in Edinburgh: one visit to Edinburgh has already cost me too dear in that invaluable particular, health; but if it should be at all possible for you to pass by Braemar, I believe you would find an attentive listener, and I can offer you a bed, a drive, and necessary food.

"If, however, you should not be able to come thus far, I can promise two things. First, I shall religiously revise what I have written, and bring out more clearly the point of view from which I regarded Thoreau. Second, I shall in the preface record your objection.

"The point of view (and I must ask you not to forget that any such short paper is essentially only a *section through* a man) was this: I desired to look at the man through his books. Thus, for instance, when I mentioned his return to the pencil-making, I did it only in passing (perhaps I was wrong), because it seemed to me not an illustration of his principles, but a brave departure from them. Thousands of such there were I do not doubt; still they might be hardly to my purpose; though, as you say so, I suppose some of them would be.

"Our difference as to 'pity,' I suspect, was a logomachy of my making. No pitiful acts, on his part, would surprise me: I know he would be more pitiful in practice than most of the whiners; but the spirit of that practice would still seem to me to be unjustly described by the word pity.

"When I try to be measured, I find myself usually suspected of a sneaking unkindness for my subject, but you may be sure, sir, I would give up most other things to be as good a man as Thoreau. Even my knowledge of him leads me thus far.

"Should you find yourself able to push on so far—it may even lie on your way—believe me your visit will be very welcome. The weather is cruel, but the place is, as I daresay you know, the very *wale* of Scotland—bar Tummelside.—Yours very sincerely,

Robert Louis Stevenson."

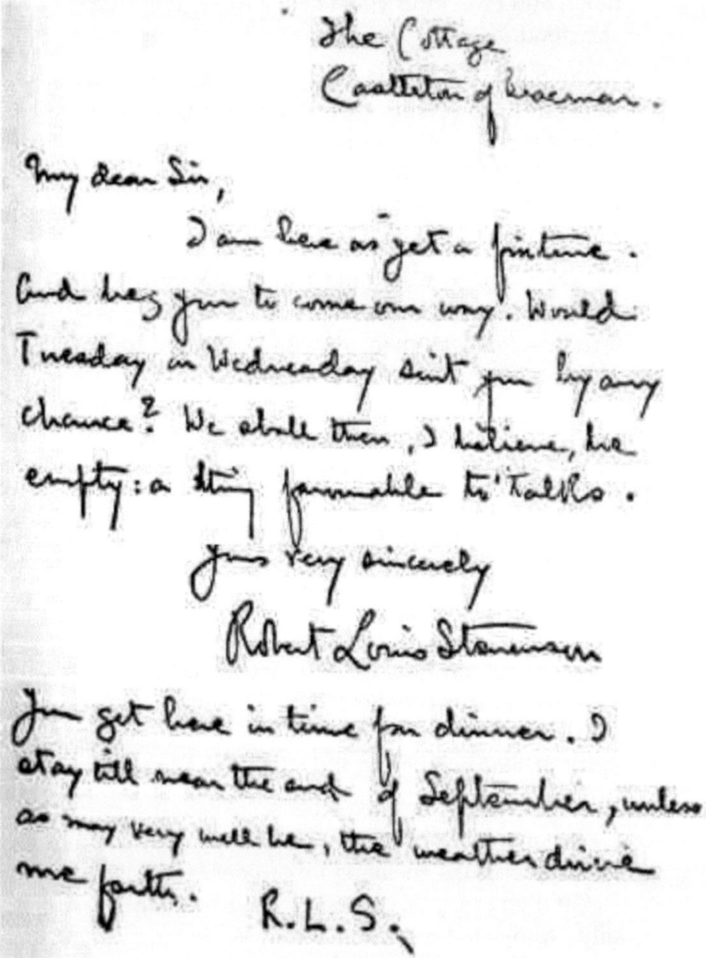

The Cottage
Castleton of Braemar.

My dear Sir,

I am here as yet a fixture. And beg you to come our way. Would Tuesday or Wednesday suit you by any chance? We shall then, I believe, be empty: a thing favourable to talks.

Yours very sincerely
Robert Louis Stevenson

You get here in time for dinner. I stay till near the end of September, unless as may very well be, the weather drive me forth.

R.L.S.

Some delay took place in my leaving London for Scotland, and hence what seemed a hitch. I wrote mentioning the reason of my delay, and expressing the fear that I might have to forego the prospect of seeing him in Braemar, as his circumstances might have altered in the meantime. In answer came this note, like so many, if not most of his, indeed, without date:—

> The Cottage, Castleton of Braemar.
> (*No date.*)
>
> "My dear Sir,—I am here as yet a fixture, and beg you to come our way. Would Tuesday or Wednesday suit you by any chance? We shall then, I believe, be empty: a thing favourable to talks. You get here in time for dinner. I stay till near the end of September, unless, as may very well be, the weather drive me forth.—Yours very sincerely, Robert Louis Stevenson."

I accordingly went to Braemar, where he and his wife and her son were staying with his father and mother.

These were red-letter days in my calendar alike on account of pleasant intercourse with his honoured father and himself. Here is my pen-and-ink portrait of R. L. Stevenson, thrown down at the time:

Mr Stevenson's is, indeed, a very picturesque and striking figure. Not so tall probably as he seems at first sight from his extreme thinness, but the pose and air could not be otherwise described than as distinguished. Head of fine type, carried well on the shoulders and in walking with the impression of being a little thrown back; long brown hair, falling from under a broadish-brimmed Spanish form of soft felt hat, Rembrandtesque; loose kind of Inverness cape when walking, and invariable velvet jacket inside the house. You would say at first sight, wherever you saw him, that he was a man of intellect, artistic and individual, wholly out of the common. His face is sensitive, full of expression, though it could not be called strictly beautiful. It is longish, especially seen in profile, and features a little irregular; the brow at once high and broad. A hint of vagary, and just a hint in the expression, is qualified by the eyes, which are set rather far apart from each other as seems, and with a most wistful, and at the same time possibly a merry impish expression arising over that, yet frank and clear, piercing, but at the same time steady, and fall on you with a gentle radiance and animation as he speaks. Romance, if with an indescribable *soupgon* of whimsicality, is marked upon him; sometimes he has the look as of the Ancient Mariner, and could fix you with his glittering e'e, and he would, as he points his sentences with a movement of his thin white forefinger, when this is not monopolised with the almost incessant cigarette. There is a faint suggestion of a hair-brained sentimental trace on his countenance, but controlled, after all, by good Scotch sense and shrewdness. In conversation he is very animated, and likes to ask questions. A favourite and characteristic attitude with him was to put his foot on a chair or stool and rest his elbow on his knee, with his chin on his hand; or to sit, or rather to half sit, half lean, on the corner of a table or desk, one of his legs swinging freely, and when anything that tickled him was said he would laugh in the heartiest manner, even at the risk of bringing on his cough, which at that time was troublesome. Often when he got animated he rose and walked about as he spoke, as if movement aided thought and expression. Though he loved Edinburgh, which was full of associations for him, he had no good word for its east winds, which to him were as death. Yet he passed one winter as a "Silverado squatter," the story of which he has inimitably told in the volume titled *The Silverado Squatters*; and he afterwards spent several winters at Davos Platz, where, as he said to me, he not only breathed good air, but learned to know with closest intimacy John Addington Symonds, who "though his books were good, was far finer and more interesting than any of his books." He needed a good deal of nursery attentions, but his invalidism was never obtrusively brought before one in any sympathy-seeking way by himself; on the contrary, a very manly, self-sustaining spirit was evident; and the amount of work which he managed to turn out even when at his worst was truly surprising.

His wife, an American lady, is highly cultured, and is herself an author. In her speech there is just the slightest suggestion of the American accent, which only made it the more pleasing to my ear. She is heart and soul devoted to her husband, proud of his achievements, and her delight is the consciousness of substantially aiding him in his enterprises.

They then had with them a boy of eleven or twelve, Samuel Lloyd Osbourne, to be much referred to later (a son of Mrs Stevenson by a former marriage), whose delight was to draw the oddest, but perhaps half intentional or unintentional caricatures, funny, in some cases, beyond expression. His room was designated the picture-gallery, and on entering I could scarce refrain from bursting into laughter, even at the general effect, and, noticing this, and that I was putting some restraint on myself out of respect for the host's feelings, Stevenson said to me with a sly wink and a gentle dig in the ribs, "It's laugh and be thankful here." On Lloyd's account simple engraving materials, types, and a small printing-press had been procured; and it was Stevenson's delight to make funny poems, stories, and morals for the engravings executed, and all would be duly printed together. Stevenson's thorough enjoyment of the picture-gallery, and his goodness to Lloyd, becoming himself a very boy for the nonce, were delightful to witness and in degree to share. Wherever they were—at Braemar, in Edinburgh, at Davos Platz, or even at Silverado—the engraving and printing went on. The mention of the picture-gallery suggests that it was out of his interest in the colour-drawing and the picture-gallery that his first published story, *Treasure Island*, grew, as we shall see.

I have some copies of the rude printing-press productions, inexpressibly quaint, grotesque, a kind of literary horse-play, yet with a certain squint-eyed, sprawling genius in it, and innocent childish Rabelaisian mirth of a sort. At all events I cannot look at the slight memorials of that time, which I still possess, without laughing afresh till my eyes are dewy. Stevenson, as I understood, began *Treasure Island* more to entertain Lloyd Osbourne than anything else; the chapters being regularly read to the family circle as they were written, and with scarcely a purpose beyond. The lad became Stevenson's trusted companion and collaborator—clearly with a touch of genius.

I have before me as I write some of these funny momentoes of that time, carefully kept, often looked at. One of them is, "*The Black Canyon; or, Wild Adventures in the Far West*: a Tale of Instruction and

Amusement for the Young, by Samuel L. Osbourne, printed by the author; Davos Platz," with the most remarkable cuts. It would not do some of the sensationalists anything but good to read it even at this day, since many points in their art are absurdly caricatured. Another is "*Moral Emblems; a Collection of Cuts and Verses*, by R. L. Stevenson, author of the *Blue Scalper*, etc., etc. Printers, S. L. Osbourne and Company, Davos Platz." Here are the lines to a rare piece of grotesque, titled *A Peak in Darien* –

"Broad-gazing on untrodden lands,
See where adventurous Cortez stands,
While in the heavens above his head,
The eagle seeks its daily bread.
How aptly fact to fact replies,
Heroes and eagles, hills and skies.
Ye, who contemn the fatted slave,
Look on this emblem and be brave."

Another, *The Elephant*, has these lines –

"See in the print how, moved by whim,
Trumpeting Jumbo, great and grim,
Adjusts his trunk, like a cravat,
To noose that individual's hat;
The Sacred Ibis in the distance,
Joys to observe his bold resistance."

R. L. Stevenson wrote from Davos Platz, in sending me *The Black Canyon*:

> "Sam sends as a present a work of his own. I hope you feel flattered, for *this is simply the first time he has ever given one away*. I have to buy my own works, I can tell you."

Later he said, in sending a second:

> "I own I have delayed this letter till I could forward the enclosed. Remembering the night at Braemar, when we visited the picture-gallery, I hope it may amuse you: you see we do some publishing hereaway."

Delightfully suggestive and highly enjoyable, too, were the meetings in the little drawing-room after dinner, when the contrasted traits of father and son came into full play—when R. L. Stevenson would sometimes draw out a new view by bold, half-paradoxical assertion, or compel advance on the point from a new quarter by a searching question couched in the simplest language, or reveal his own latest conviction finally, by a few sentences as nicely rounded off as though they had been written, while he rose and gently moved about, as his habit was, in the course of those more extended remarks. Then a chapter or two of *The Sea-Cook* would be read, with due pronouncement on the main points by one or other of the family audience.

The reading of the book is one thing. It was quite another thing to hear Stevenson as he stood reading it aloud, with his hand stretched out holding the manuscript, and his body gently swaying as a kind of rhythmical commentary on the story. His fine voice, clear and keen it some of its tones, had a wonderful power of inflection and variation, and when he came to stand in the place of Silver you could almost have imagined you saw the great one-legged John Silver, joyous-eyed, on the rolling sea. Yes, to read it in print was good, but better yet to hear Stevenson read it.

CHAPTER II – *TREASURE ISLAND* AND SOME REMINISCENCES

When I left Braemar, I carried with me a considerable portion of the MS. of *Treasure Island,* with an outline of the rest of the story. It originally bore the odd title of *The Sea-Cook,* and, as I have told before, I showed it to Mr Henderson, the proprietor of the *Young Folks' Paper,* who came to an arrangement with Mr Stevenson, and the story duly appeared in its pages, as well as the two which succeeded it.

Stevenson himself in his article in *The Idler* for August 1894 (reprinted in *My First Book* volume and in a late volume of the *Edinburgh Edition*) has recalled some of the circumstances connected with this visit of mine to Braemar, as it bore on the destination of *Treasure Island*:

> "And now, who should come dropping in, *ex machinb,* but Dr Japp, like the disguised prince, who is to bring down the curtain upon peace and happiness in the last act; for he carried in his pocket, not a horn or a talisman, but a publisher, in fact, ready to unearth new writers for my old friend Mr Henderson's *Young Folks.* Even the ruthlessness of a united family recoiled before the extreme measure of inflicting on our guest the mutilated members of *The Sea-Cook;* at the same time, we would by no means stop our readings, and accordingly the tale was begun again at the beginning, and solemnly redelivered for the benefit of Dr Japp. From that moment on, I have thought highly of his critical faculty; for when he left us, he carried away the manuscript in his portmanteau.
>
> "*Treasure Island* – it was Mr Henderson who deleted the first title, *The Sea-Cook* – appeared duly in *Young Folks,* where it figured in the ignoble midst without woodcuts, and attracted not the least attention. I did not care. I liked the tale myself, for

much the same reason as my father liked the beginning: it was my kind of picturesque. I was not a little proud of John Silver also; and to this day rather admire that smooth and formidable adventurer. What was infinitely more exhilarating, I had passed a landmark. I had finished a tale and written The End upon my manuscript, as I had not done since *The Pentland Rising*, when I was a boy of sixteen, not yet at college. In truth, it was so by a lucky set of accidents: had not Dr Japp come on his visit, had not the tale flowed from me with singular ease, it must have been laid aside, like its predecessors, and found a circuitous and unlamented way to the fire. Purists may suggest it would have been better so. I am not of that mind. The tale seems to have given much pleasure, and it brought (or was the means of bringing) fire, food, and wine to a deserving family in which I took an interest. I need scarcely say I mean my own."

He himself gives a goodly list of the predecessors which had "found a circuitous and unlamented way to the fire":

> "As soon as I was able to write, I became a good friend to the paper-makers. Reams upon reams must have gone to the making of *Rathillet*, *The Pentland Rising*, *The King's Pardon* (otherwise *Park Whitehead*), *Edward Daven*, *A Country Dance*, and *A Vendetta in the West*. *Rathillet* was attempted before fifteen, *The Vendetta* at twenty-nine, and the succession of defeats lasted unbroken till I was thirty-one."

Another thing I carried from Braemar with me which I greatly prize—this was a copy of *Christianity confirmed by Jewish and Heathen Testimony*, by Mr Stevenson's father, with his autograph signature and many of his own marginal notes. He had thought deeply on many subjects—theological, scientific, and social—and had recorded, I am afraid, but the smaller half of his thoughts and speculations. Several days in the mornings, before R. L. Stevenson was able to face the somewhat "snell" air of the hills, I had long walks with the old gentleman, when we also had long talks on many subjects—the liberalising of the Scottish Church, educational reform, etc.; and, on one occasion, a statement of his reason, because of the subscription, for never having become an elder. That he had in some small measure enjoyed my society, as I certainly had much enjoyed his, was borne out by a letter which I received from the son in reply to one I had written, saying that surely his father had never meant to present me at the last moment on my leaving by coach with that volume, with his name on it, and with pencilled notes here and there, but had merely given it me to read and return. In the circumstances I may perhaps be excused quoting from a letter dated Castleton of Braemar, September 1881, in illustration of what I have said—

> "My dear Dr Japp,—My father has gone, but I think I may take it upon me to ask you to keep the book. Of all things you could do to endear yourself to me you have done the best, for, from your letter, you have taken a fancy to my father.
>
> "I do not know how to thank you for your kind trouble in the matter of *The Sea-Cook*, but I am not unmindful. My health is still poorly, and I have added intercostal rheumatism—a new attraction, which sewed me up nearly double for two days, and still gives me 'a list to starboard'—let us be ever nautical. . . . I do not think with the start I have, there will be any difficulty in letting Mr Henderson go ahead whenever he likes. I will write my story up to its legitimate conclusion, and then we shall be in a position to judge whether a sequel would be desirable, and I myself would then know better about its practicability from the story-telling point of view.—Yours very sincerely, Robert Louis Stevenson."

A little later came the following:—

> "The Cottage, Castleton of Braemar.
> (*No date*.)

"My dear Dr Japp,—Herewith go nine chapters. I have been a little seedy; and the two last that I have written seem to me on a false venue; hence the smallness of the batch. I have now, I hope, in the three last sent, turned the corner, with no great amount of dulness.

"The map, with all its names, notes, soundings, and things, should make, I believe, an admirable advertisement for the story. Eh?

"I hope you got a telegram and letter I forwarded after you to Dinnat.—Believe me, yours very sincerely, Robert Louis Stevenson."

In the afternoon, if fine and dry, we went walking, and Stevenson would sometimes tell us stories of his short experience at the Scottish Bar, and of his first and only brief. I remember him contrasting that with his experiences as an engineer with Bob Bain, who, as manager, was then superintending the building of a breakwater. Of that time, too, he told the choicest stories, and especially of how, against all orders, he bribed Bob with five shillings to let him go down in the diver's dress. He gave us a splendid description—finer, I think, than even that in his *Memories*—of his sensations on the sea-bottom, which seems to have interested him as deeply, and suggested as many strange fancies, as anything which he ever came across on the surface. But the possibility of enterprises of this sort ended—Stevenson lost his interest in engineering.

XI chapters now,
as I have revised
the 10.

The Cottage
Castleton of Braemar.

My dear Dr Japp,

Herewith go IX chapters. I have been a little seedy; and the two last that I have written seem to me on a false scent; hence the smallness of the batch.

I have now, I hope, in the 3 last sent, turned the corner from the introduction to the story, which was the hitch, with no too great amount of dulness.

The map, with all its names, notes, soundings and things, should make, I believe, an admirable advertisement for the story: eh?

I hope you got a telegram and letter I forwarded after you to Dunnet.

Believe me.

Yours sincerely

Robert Louis Stevenson

Stevenson's father had, indeed, been much exercised in his day by theological questions and difficulties, and though he remained a staunch adherent of the Established Church of Scotland he knew well and practically what is meant by the term "accommodation," as it is used by theologians in reference to creeds and formulas; for he had over and over again, because of the strict character of the subscription required from elders of the Scottish Church declined, as I have said, to accept the office. In a very express sense you could see that he bore the marks of his past in many ways—a quick, sensitive, in some ways even a fantastic-minded man, yet with a strange solidity and common-sense amid it all, just as though ferns with the veritable fairies' seed were to grow out of a common stone wall. He looked like a man who had not been without sleepless nights—without troubles, sorrows, and perplexities, and even yet, had not wholly risen above some of them, or the results of them. His voice was "low and sweet"—with just a possibility in it of rising to a shrillish key. A sincere and faithful man, who had walked very demurely through life, though with a touch of sudden, bright, quiet humour and fancy, every now and then crossing the grey of his characteristic pensiveness or melancholy, and drawing effect from it. He was most frank and genial with me, and I greatly honour his memory. [2]

Thomas Stevenson, with a strange, sad smile, told me how much of a disappointment, in the first stage, at all events, Louis (he always called his son Louis at home), had caused him, by failing to follow up his profession at the Scottish Bar. How much he had looked forward, after the engineering was abandoned, to his devoting himself to the work of the Parliament House (as the Hall of the Chief Court is called in Scotland, from the building having been while yet there was a Scottish Parliament the place where it sat), though truly one cannot help feeling how much Stevenson's very air and figure would have been out of keeping among the bewigged, pushing, sharp-set, hard-featured, and even red-faced and red-nosed (some of them, at any rate) company, who daily walked the Parliament House, and talked and gossiped there, often of other things than law and equity. "Well, yes, perhaps it was all for the best," he said, with a sigh, on my having interjected the remark that R. L. Stevenson was wielding far more influence than he ever could have done as a Scottish counsel, even though he had risen rapidly in his profession, and become Lord-Advocate or even a judge.

There was, indeed, a very pathetic kind of harking back on the might-have-beens when I talked with him on this subject. He had reconciled himself in a way to the inevitable, and, like a sensible man, was now inclined to make the most and the best of it. The marriage, which, on the report of it, had been but a new disappointment to him, had, as if by magic, been transformed into a blessing in his mind and his wife's by personal contact with Fanny Van der Griff Stevenson, which no one who ever met her could wonder at; but, nevertheless, his dream of seeing his only son walking in the pathways of the Stevensons, and adorning a profession in Edinburgh, and so winning new and welcome laurels for the family and the name, was still present with him constantly, and by contrast, he was depressed with contemplation of the real state of the case, when, as I have said, I pointed out to him, as more than once I did, what an influence his son was wielding now, not only over those near to him, but throughout the world, compared with what could have come to him as a lighthouse engineer, however successful, or it may be as a briefless advocate or barrister, walking, hardly in glory and in joy, the Hall of the Edinburgh Parliament House. And when I pictured the yet greater influence that was sure to come to him, he only shook his head with that smile which tells of hopes long-cherished and lost at last, and of resignation gained, as though at stern duty's call and an honest desire for the good of those near and dear to him. It moved me more than I can say, and always in the midst of it he adroitly, and somewhat abruptly, changed the subject. Such penalties do parents often pay for the honour of giving geniuses to the world. Here, again, it may be true, "the individual withers but the world is more and more."

The impression of a kind of tragic fatality was but added to when Stevenson would speak of his father in such terms of love and admiration as quite moved one, of his desire to please him, of his highest respect and gratitude to him, and pride in having such a father. It was most characteristic that when, in his travels in America, he met a gentleman who expressed plainly his keen disappointment on learning that he had but been introduced to the son and not to the father—to the as yet but budding author—and not to the builder of the great lighthouse beacons that constantly saved mariners from shipwreck round many stormy coasts, he should record the incident, as his readers will remember, with such a strange mixture of a pride and filial gratitude, and half humorous humiliation. Such is the penalty a son of genius often pays in heart-throbs for the inability to do aught else but follow his destiny—follow his star, even though as Dante says:—

> "Se tu segui tua stella
> Non puoi fallire a glorioso porto." [3]

What added a keen thrill as of quivering flesh exposed, was that Thomas Stevenson on one side was exactly the man to appreciate such attainments and work in another, and I often wondered how far the sense of Edinburgh propriety and worldly estimates did weigh with him here.

Mr Stevenson mentioned to me a peculiar fact which has since been noted by his son, that, notwithstanding the kind of work he had so successfully engaged in, he was no mathematician, and had to submit his calculations to another to be worked out in definite mathematical formulf. Thomas Stevenson gave one the impression of a remarkably sweet, great personality, grave, anxious, almost morbidly forecasting, yet full of childlike hope and ready affection, but, perhaps, so earnestly taken up with some points as to exaggerate their importance and be too self-conscious and easily offended in respect to them. But there was no affectation in him. He was simple-minded, sincere to the core; most kindly, homely, hospitable, much intent on brotherly offices. He had the Scottish *perfervidum* too—he could tolerate nothing mean or creeping; and his eye would lighten and glance in a striking manner when such was spoken of. I have since heard that his charities were very extensive, and dispensed in the most hidden and secret ways. He acted here on the Scripture direction, "Let not thy left hand know what thy right hand doeth." He was much exercised when I saw him about some defects, as he held, in the methods of Scotch education (for he was a true lover of youth, and cared more for character being formed than for heads being merely crammed). Sagacious, with fine forecast, with a high ideal, and yet up to a certain point a most tolerant temper, he was a fine specimen of the Scottish gentleman. His son tells that, as he was engaged in work calculated to benefit the world and to save life, he would not for long take out a patent for his inventions, and thus lost immense sums. I can well believe that: it seems quite in keeping with my impressions of the man. There was nothing stolid or selfishly absorbed in him. He bore the marks of deep, true, honest feeling, true benevolence, and open-handed generosity, and despite the son's great pen-craft, and inventive power, would have forgiven my saying that sometimes I have had a doubt whether the father was not, after all, the greater man of the two, though certainly not, like the hero of *In Memoriam*, moulded "in colossal calm."

In theological matters, in which Thomas Stevenson had been much and deeply exercised, he held very strong views, leading decisively to ultra-Calvinism; but, as I myself could well sympathise with such views, if I did not hold them, knowing well the strange ways in which they had gone to form grand, if sometimes sternly forbidding characters, there were no cross-purposes as there might have been with some on that subject. And always I felt I had an original character and a most interesting one to study.

This is another very characteristic letter to me from Davos Platz:

> "Chalet Buol, Davos, Grisons,
> Switzerland. (*No date.*)
>
> "My dear Dr Japp,—You must think me a forgetful rogue, as indeed I am; for I have but now told my publisher to send you a copy of the *Familiar Studies*. However, I own I have delayed this letter till I could send you the enclosed. Remembering the night at Braemar, when we visited the picture-gallery, I hoped they might amuse you.
>
> "You see we do some publishing hereaway.
>
> "With kind regards, believe me, always yours faithfully,
>
> Robert Louis Stevenson."
>
> "I shall hope to see you in town in May."

The enclosed was the second series of *Moral Emblems*, by R. L. Stevenson, printed by Samuel Osbourne. My answer to this letter brought the following:

"Chalet-Buol, Davos,
April 1*st*, 1882.

"My dear Dr Japp,—A good day to date this letter, which is, in fact, a confession of incapacity. During my wife's wretched illness—or I should say the worst of it, for she is not yet rightly well—I somewhat lost my head, and entirely lost a great quire of corrected proofs. This is one of the results: I hope there are none more serious. I was never so sick of any volume as I was of that; I was continually receiving fresh proofs with fresh infinitesimal difficulties. I was ill; I did really fear, for my wife was worse than ill. Well, 'tis out now; and though I have already observed several carelessnesses myself, and now here is another of your finding—of which indeed, I ought to be ashamed—it will only justify the sweeping humility of the preface.

"Symonds was actually dining with us when your letter came, and I communicated your remarks, which pleased him. He is a far better and more interesting thing than his books.

"The elephant was my wife's, so she is proportionately elate you should have picked it out for praise from a collection, let us add, so replete with the highest qualities of art.

"My wicked carcass, as John Knox calls it, holds together wonderfully. In addition to many other things, and a volume of travel, I find I have written since December ninety Cornhill pp. of Magazine work—essays and stories—40,000 words; and I am none the worse—I am better. I begin to hope I may, if not outlive this wolverine upon my shoulders, at least carry him bravely like Symonds or

Alexander Pope. I begin to take a pride in that hope.

"I shall be much interested to see your criticisms: you might perhaps send them on to me. I believe you know that I am not dangerous—one folly I have not—I am not touchy under criticism.

"Sam and my wife both beg to be remembered, and Sam also sends as a present a work of his own.—Yours very sincerely,

Robert Louis Stevenson."

As indicating the estimate of many of the good Edinburgh people of Stevenson and the Stevensons that still held sway up to so late a date as 1893, I will here extract two characteristic passages from the letters of the friend and correspondent of these days just referred to, and to whom I had sent a copy of the *Atalanta* Magazine, with an article of mine on Stevenson.

> "If you can excuse the garrulity of age, I can tell you one or two things about Louis Stevenson, his father and even his grandfather, which you may work up some other day, as you have so deftly embedded in the *Atalanta* article that small remark on his acting. Your paper is pleasant and modest: most of R. L. Stevenson's admirers are inclined to lay it on far too thick. That he is a genius we all admit; but his genius, if fine, is limited. For example, he cannot paint (or at least he never has painted) a woman. No more could Fettes Douglas, skilful artist though he was in his own special line, and I shall tell you a remark of Russel's thereon some day. [4] There are women in his books, but there is none of the beauty and subtlety of womanhood in them.
>
> "R. L. Stevenson I knew well as a lad and often met him and talked with him. He acted in private theatricals got up by the late Professor Fleeming Jenkin. But he had then, as always, a pretty guid

conceit o' himsel'—which his clique have done nothing to check. His father and his grandfather (I have danced with his mother before her marriage) I knew better; but 'the family theologian,' as some of R. L. Stevenson's friends dabbed his father, was a very touchy theologian, and denounced any one who in the least differed from his extreme Calvinistic views. I came under his lash most unwittingly in this way myself. But for this twist, he was a good fellow—kind and hospitable—and a really able man in his profession. His father-in-law, R. L. Stevenson's maternal grandfather, was the Rev. Dr Balfour, minister of Colinton—one of the finest-looking old men I ever saw—tall, upright, and ruddy at eighty. But he was marvellously feeble as a preacher, and often said things that were deliciously, unconsciously, unintentionally laughable, if not witty. We were near Colinton for some years; and Mr Russell (of the *Scotsman*), who once attended the Parish Church with us, was greatly tickled by Balfour discoursing on the story of Joseph and Potiphar's wife, remarking that Mrs P---'s conduct was 'highly improper'!"

The estimate of R. L. Stevenson was not and could not be final in this case, for *Weir of Hermiston* and *Catriona* were yet unwritten, not to speak of others, but the passages reflect a certain side of Edinburgh opinion, illustrating the old Scripture doctrine that a prophet has honour everywhere but in his own country. And the passages themselves bear evidence that I violate no confidence then, for they were given to me to be worked into any after-effort I might make on Stevenson. My friend was a good and an acute critic who had done some acceptable literary work in his day.

CHAPTER III – THE CHILD FATHER OF THE MAN

R. L. Stevenson was born on 13th November 1850, the very year of the death of his grandfather, Robert Stevenson, whom he has so finely celebrated. As a mere child he gave token of his character. As soon as he could read, he was keen for books, and, before very long, had read all the story-books he could lay hands on; and, when the stock ran out, he would go and look in at all the shop windows within reach, and try to piece out the stories from the bits exposed in open pages and the woodcuts.

He had a nurse of very remarkable character – evidently a paragon – who deeply influenced him and did much to form his young mind – Alison Cunningham, who, in his juvenile lingo, became "Cumy," and who not only was never forgotten, but to the end was treated as his "second mother." In his dedication of his *Child's Garden of Verses* to her, he says:

> "My second mother, my first wife,
> The angel of my infant life."

Her copy of *Kidnapped* was inscribed to her by the hand of Stevenson, thus:

> "To Cumy, from her boy, the author.
> Skerryvore, 18*thJuly* 1888."

Skerryvore was the name of Stevenson's Bournemouth home, so named after one of the Stevenson lighthouses. His first volume, *An Inland Voyage* has this pretty dedication, inscribed in a neat, small hand:

> "My dear Cumy, – If you had not taken so much trouble with me all the years of my childhood, this little book would never have been written. Many a long night you sat up with me when I was ill. I wish I could hope, by way of return, to amuse a single evening for you with my little book. But whatever you think of it, I know you will think kindly of

The Author."

"Cumy" was perhaps the most influential teacher Stevenson had. What she and his mother taught took effect and abode with him, which was hardly the case with any other of his teachers.

> "In contrast to Goethe," says Mr Baildon, "Stevenson was but little affected by his relations to women, and, when this point is fully gone into, it will probably be found that his mother and nurse in childhood, and his wife and step-daughter in later life, are about the only women who seriously influenced either his character or his art." (p. 32).

When Mr Kelman is celebrating Stevenson for the consistency and continuity of his undogmatic religion, he is almost throughout celebrating "Cumy" and her influence, though unconsciously. Here, again, we have an apt and yet more striking illustration, after that of the good Lord Shaftesbury and many others, of the deep and lasting effect a good and earnest woman, of whom the world may never hear, may have had upon a youngster of whom all the world shall hear. When Mr Kelman says that "the religious element in Stevenson was not a thing of late growth, but an integral part and vital interest of his life," he but points us back to the earlier religious influences to which he had been effectually subject. "His faith was not for himself alone, and the phases of Christianity which it has asserted are peculiarly suited to the spiritual needs of many in the present time."

We should not lay so much weight as Mr Kelman does on the mere number of times "the Divine name" is found in Stevenson's writings, but there is something in such confessions as the following to his father, when he was, amid hardship and illness, in Paris in 1878:

> "Still I believe in myself and my fellow-men and the God who made us all. . . . I am lonely and sick and out of heart. Well, I still hope; I still believe; I still see the good in the inch, and cling to it. It is not much, perhaps, but it is always something."

Yes, "Cumy" was a very effective teacher, whose influence and teaching long remained. His other teachers, however famous and highly gifted, did not attain to such success with him. And because of this non-success they blamed him, as is usual. He was fond of playing truant—declared, indeed, that he was about as methodic a truant as ever could have existed. He much loved to go on long wanderings by himself on the Pentland Hills and read about the Covenanters, and while yet a youth of sixteen he wrote *The Pentland Rising*—a pamphlet in size and a piece of fine work—which was duly published, is now scarce, and fetches a high price. He had made himself thoroughly familiar with all the odd old corners of Edinburgh—John Knox's haunts and so on, all which he has turned to account in essays, descriptions and in stories—especially in *Catriona*. When a mere youth at school, as he tells us himself, he had little or no desire to carry off prizes and do just as other boys did; he was always wishing to observe, and to see, and try things for himself—was, in fact, in the eyes of schoolmasters and tutors something of an *idler*, with splendid gifts which he would not rightly apply. He was applying them rightly, though not in their way. It is not only in his *Apology for Idlers* that this confession is made, but elsewhere, as in his essay on *A College Magazine*, where he says, "I was always busy on my own private end, which was to learn to write. I kept always two books in my pocket, one to read and one to write in!"

When he went to College it was still the same—he tells us in the funniest way how he managed to wheedle a certificate for Greek out of Professor Blackie, though the Professor owned "his face was not familiar to him"! He fared very differently when, afterwards his father, eager that he should follow his profession, got him to enter the civil engineering class under Professor Fleeming Jenkin. He still stuck to his old courses—wandering about, and, in sheltered corners, writing in the open air, and was not present in class more than a dozen times. When the session was ended he went up to try for a certificate from Fleeming Jenkin. "No, no, Mr Stevenson," said the Professor; "I might give it in a doubtful case, but yours is not doubtful: you have not kept my classes." And the most characteristic thing—honourable to both men—is to come; for this was the beginning of a friendship which grew and strengthened and is finally celebrated in the younger man's sketch of the elder. He learned from Professor Fleeming Jenkin, perhaps unconsciously, more of the *humaniores*, than consciously he did of engineering. A friend of mine, who knew well both the Stevenson family and the Balfours, to which R. L. Stevenson's mother belonged, recalls, as we have seen, his acting in the private theatricals that were got up by the Professor, and adds, "He was then a very handsome fellow, and looked splendidly as Sir Charles Pomander, and essayed, not wholly without success, Sir Peter Teazle," which one can well believe, no less than that he acted such parts splendidly as well as looked them.

Longman's Magazine, immediately after his death, published the following poem, which took a very pathetic touch from the circumstances of its appearance—the more that, while it imaginatively and finely commemorated these days of truant wanderings, it showed the ruling passion for home and the old haunts, strongly and vividly, even not unnigh to death:

> "The tropics vanish, and meseems that I,
> From Halkerside, from topmost Allermuir,
> Or steep Caerketton, dreaming gaze again.
> Far set in fields and woods, the town I see
> Spring gallant from the shallows of her smoke,
> Cragg'd, spired, and turreted, her virgin fort
> Beflagg'd. About, on seaward drooping hills,
> New folds of city glitter. Last, the Forth
> Wheels ample waters set with sacred isles,
> And populous Fife smokes with a score of towns,
> There, on the sunny frontage of a hill,
> Hard by the house of kings, repose the dead,
> My dead, the ready and the strong of word.
> Their works, the salt-encrusted, still survive;
> The sea bombards their founded towers; the night
> Thrills pierced with their strong lamps. The artificers,
> One after one, here in this grated cell,
> Where the rain erases and the rust consumes,
> Fell upon lasting silence. Continents
> And continental oceans intervene;
> A sea uncharted, on a lampless isle,
> Environs and confines their wandering child

In vain. The voice of generations dead
Summons me, sitting distant, to arise,
My numerous footsteps nimbly to retrace,
And all mutation over, stretch me down
In that denoted city of the dead."

CHAPTER IV – HEREDITY ILLUSTRATED

At first sight it would seem hard to trace any illustration of the doctrine of heredity in the case of this master of romance. George Eliot's dictum that we are, each one of us, but an omnibus carrying down the traits of our ancestors, does not appear at all to hold here. This fanciful realist, this ndive-wistful humorist, this dreamy mystical casuist, crossed by the innocent bohemian, this serious and genial essayist, in whom the deep thought was hidden by the gracious play of wit and phantasy, came, on the father's side, of a stock of what the world regarded as a quiet, ingenious, demure, practical, home-keeping people. In his rich colour, originality, and graceful air, it is almost as though the bloom of japonica came on a rich old orchard apple-tree, all out of season too. Those who go hard on heredity would say, perhaps, that he was the result of some strange back-stroke. But, on closer examination, we need not go so far. His grandfather, Robert Stevenson, the great lighthouse-builder, the man who reared the iron-bound pillar on the destructive Bell Rock, and set life-saving lights there, was very intent on his professional work, yet he had his ideal, and romantic, and adventurous side. In the delightful sketch which his famous grandson gave of him, does he not tell of the joy Robert Stevenson had on the annual voyage in the *Lighthouse Yacht*–how it was looked forward to, yearned for, and how, when he had Walter Scott on board, his fund of story and reminiscence all through the tour never failed–how Scott drew upon it in *The Pirate* and the notes to *The Pirate*, and with what pride Robert Stevenson preserved the lines Scott wrote in the lighthouse album at the Bell Rock on that occasion:

"PHAROS LOQUITUR

"Far in the bosom of the deep
O'er these wild shelves my watch I keep,
A ruddy gem of changeful light
Bound on the dusky brow of night.
The seaman bids my lustre hail,
And scorns to strike his timorous sail."

And how in 1850 the old man, drawing nigh unto death, was with the utmost difficulty dissuaded from going the voyage once more, and was found furtively in his room packing his portmanteau in spite of the protests of all his family, and would have gone but for the utter weakness of death.

His father was also a splendid engineer; was full of invention and devoted to his profession, but he, too, was not without his romances, and even vagaries. He loved a story, was a fine teller of stories, used to sit at night and spin the most wondrous yarns, a man of much reserve, yet also of much power in discourse, with an aptness and felicity in the use of phrases—so much so, as his son tells, that on his deathbed, when his power of speech was passing from him, and he couldn't articulate the right word, he was silent rather than use the wrong one. I shall never forget how in these early morning walks at Braemar, finding me sympathetic, he unbent with the air of a man who had unexpectedly found something he had sought, and was fairly confidential.

On the mother's side our author came of ministers. His maternal grandfather, the Rev. Dr Balfour of Colinton, was a man of handsome presence, tall, venerable-looking, and not without a mingled authority and humour of his own—no very great preacher, I have heard, but would sometimes bring a smile to the faces of his hearers by very naove and original ways of putting things. R. L. Stevenson quaintly tells a story of how his grandfather when he had physic to take, and was indulged in a sweet afterwards, yet would not allow the child to have a sweet because he had not had the physic. A veritable Calvinist in daily action—from him, no doubt, our subject drew much of his interest in certain directions—John Knox, Scottish history, the '15 and the '45, and no doubt much that justifies the line "something of shorter-catechist," as applied by Henley to Stevenson among very contrasted traits indeed.

But strange truly are the interblendings of race, and the way in which traits of ancestors reappear, modifying and transforming each other. The gardener knows what can be done by grafts and buddings; but more wonderful far than anything there, are the mysterious blendings and outbursts of what is old and forgotten, along with what is wholly new and strange, and all going to produce often what we call sometimes eccentricity, and sometimes originality and genius.

Mr J. F. George, in *Scottish Notes and Queries*, wrote as follows on Stevenson's inheritances and indebtedness to certain of his ancestors:

> "About 1650, James Balfour, one of the Principal Clerks of the Court of Session, married Bridget, daughter of Chalmers of Balbaithan, Keithhall, and that estate was for some time in the name of Balfour. His son, James Balfour of Balbaithan, Merchant and Magistrate of Edinburgh, paid poll-tax in 1696, but by 1699 the land had been sold. This was probably due to the fact that Balfour was one of the Governors of the Darien Company. His grandson, James Balfour of Pilrig (1705-1795), sometime Professor of Moral Philosophy in Edinburgh University, whose portrait is sketched in *Catriona*, also made a Garioch [Aberdeenshire district] marriage, his wife being Cecilia, fifth daughter of Sir John Elphinstone, second baronet of Logie (Elphinstone) and Sheriff of Aberdeen, by Mary, daughter of Sir Gilbert Elliot, first baronet of Minto.
>
> "Referring to the Minto descent, Stevenson claims to have 'shaken a spear in the Debatable Land and shouted the slogan of the Elliots.' He evidently knew little or nothing of his relations on the Elphinstone side. The Logie Elphinstones were a cadet branch of Glack, an estate acquired by Nicholas Elphinstone in 1499. William Elphinstone, a younger son of James of Glack, and Elizabeth Wood of Bonnyton, married Margaret Forbes, and was father of Sir James Elphinstone, Bart., of Logie, so created in 1701. . . .
>
> "Stevenson would have been delighted to acknowledge his relationship, remote though it was, to 'the Wolf of Badenoch,' who burned Elgin Cathedral without the Earl of Kildare's excuse that he thought the Bishop was in it; and to the Wolf's

son, the Victor of Harlaw [and] to his nephew 'John O'Coull,' Constable of France. . . . Also among Tusitala's kin may be noted, in addition to the later Gordons of Gight, the Tiger Earl of Crawford, familiarly known as 'Earl Beardie,' the 'Wicked Master' of the same line, who was fatally stabbed by a Dundee cobbler 'for taking a stoup of drink from him'; Lady Jean Lindsay, who ran away with 'a common jockey with the horn,' and latterly became a beggar; David Lindsay, the last Laird of Edzell [a lichtsome Lindsay fallen on evil days], who ended his days as hostler at a Kirkwall inn, and 'Mussel Mou'ed Charlie,' the Jacobite ballad-singer.

"Stevenson always believed that he had a strong spiritual affinity to Robert Fergusson. It is more than probable that there was a distant maternal affinity as well. Margaret Forbes, the mother of Sir James Elphinstone, the purchaser of Logie, has not been identified, but it is probable she was of the branch of the Tolquhon Forbeses who previously owned Logie. Fergusson's mother, Elizabeth Forbes, was the daughter of a Kildrummy tacksman, who by constant tradition is stated to have been of the house of Tolquhon. It would certainly be interesting if this suggested connection could be proved." [5]

"From his Highland ancestors," says the *Quarterly Review*, "Louis drew the strain of Celtic melancholy with all its perils and possibilities, and its kinship, to the mood of day-dreaming, which has flung over so many of his pages now the vivid light wherein figures imagined grew as real as flesh and blood, and yet, again, the ghostly, strange, lonesome, and stinging mist under whose spell we see the world bewitched, and every object quickens with a throb of infectious terror."

Here, as in many other cases, we see how the traits of ancestry reappear and transform other strains, strangely the more remote often being the strongest and most persistent and wonderful.

"It is through his father, strange as it may seem," says Mr Baildon, "that Stevenson gets the Celtic elements so marked in his person, character, and genius; for his father's pedigree runs back to the Highland clan Macgregor, the kin of Rob Roy. Stevenson thus drew in Celtic strains from both sides—from the Balfours and the Stevensons alike—and in his strange, dreamy, beautiful, and often far-removed fancies we have the finest and most effective witness of it."

Mr William Archer, in his own characteristic way, has brought the inheritances from the two sides of the house into more direct contact and contrast in an article he wrote in *The Daily Chronicle* on the appearance of the *Letters to Family and Friends*.

> "These letters show," he says, "that Stevenson's was not one of those sunflower temperaments which turn by instinct, not effort, towards the light, and are, as Mr Francis Thompson puts it, 'heartless and happy, lackeying their god.' The strains of his heredity were very curiously, but very clearly, mingled. It may surprise some readers to find him speaking of 'the family evil, despondency,' but he spoke with knowledge. He inherited from his father not only a stern Scottish intentness on the moral aspect of life ('I would rise from the dead to preach'), but a marked disposition to melancholy and hypochondria. From his mother, on the other hand, he derived, along with his physical frailty, a resolute and cheery stoicism. These two elements in his nature fought many a hard fight, and the besieging forces from without—ill-health, poverty, and at one time family dissensions—were by no means without allies in the inner citadel of his soul. His spirit was courageous in the truest sense of the word: by effort and conviction, not by temperamental insensibility to fear. It is clear that there was a period in his life

(and that before the worst of his bodily ills came upon him) when he was often within measurable distance of Carlylean gloom. He was twenty-four when he wrote thus, from Swanston, to Mrs Sitwell:

"'It is warmer a bit; but my body is most decrepit, and I can just manage to be cheery and tread down hypochondria under foot by work. I lead such a funny life, utterly without interest or pleasure outside of my work: nothing, indeed, but work all day long, except a short walk alone on the cold hills, and meals, and a couple of pipes with my father in the evening. It is surprising how it suits me, and how happy I keep.'

"This is the serenity which arises, not from the absence of fuliginous elements in the character, but from a potent smoke-consuming faculty, and an inflexible will to use it. Nine years later he thus admonishes his backsliding parent:

"'My dear Mother,—I give my father up. I give him a parable: that the Waverley novels are better reading for every day than the tragic *Life*. And he takes it back-side foremost, and shakes his head, and is gloomier than ever. Tell him that I give him up. I don't want no such a parent. This is not the man for my money. I do not call that by the name of religion which fills a man with bile. I write him a whole letter, bidding him beware of extremes, and telling him that his gloom is gallows-worthy; and I get back an answer—. Perish the thought of it.

"'Here am I on the threshold of another year, when, according to all human foresight, I should long ago have been resolved into my elements: here am I, who you were persuaded was born to disgrace you—and, I will do you the justice to add, on no such insufficient grounds—no very burning discredit when all is done; here am I married, and the marriage recognised to be a blessing of the first order. A1 at Lloyd's. There is he, at his not first youth, able to take more exercise than I at thirty-three, and gaining a stone's weight, a thing of which I am incapable. There are you; has the man no gratitude? . . .

"'Even the Shorter Catechism, not the merriest epitome of religion, and a work exactly as pious although not quite so true as the multiplication table—even that dry-as-dust epitome begins with a heroic note. What is man's chief end? Let him study that; and ask himself if to refuse to enjoy God's kindest gifts is in the spirit indicated.'

"As may be judged from this half-playful, half-serious remonstrance, Stevenson's relation to his parents was eminently human and beautiful. The family dissensions above alluded to belonged only to a short but painful period, when the father could not reconcile himself to the discovery that the son had ceased to accept the formulas of Scottish Calvinism. In the eyes of the older man such heterodoxy was for the moment indistinguishable from atheism; but he soon arrived at a better understanding of his son's position. Nothing appears more unmistakably in these letters than the ingrained theism of Stevenson's way of thought. The poet, the romancer within him, revolted from the conception of formless force. A personal deity was a necessary character in the drama, as he conceived it. And his morality, though (or inasmuch as) it dwelt more on positive kindness than on negative lawlessness, was, as he often insisted, very much akin to the morality of the New Testament."

Anyway it is clear that much in the interminglings of blood we *can* trace, may go to account for not a little in Stevenson. His peculiar interest in the enormities of old-time feuds, the excesses, the jealousies, the queer psychological puzzles, the desire to work on the outlying and morbid, and even the unallowed and unhallowed, for purposes of romance—the delight in dealing with revelations of primitive feeling and the out-bursts of the mere natural man always strangely checked and diverted by the uprise of other tendencies to the dreamy, impalpable, vague, weird and horrible. There was the undoubted Celtic element in him underlying what seemed foreign to it, the disregard of conventionality in one phase, and the falling under it in another—the reaction and the retreat from what had attracted and interested him, and then the return upon it, as with added zest because of the retreat. The confessed Hedonist, enjoying life and boasting of it just a little, and yet the Puritan in him, as it were, all the time eyeing himself as from some loophole of retreat, and then commenting on his own behaviour as a Hedonist and Bohemian. This clearly was not what most struck Beerbohm Tree, during the time he was in close contact with Stevenson, while arranging the production of *Beau Austin* at the Haymarket Theatre, for he sees, or confesses to seeing, only one side, and that the most assertive, and in a sense, unreal one:

> "Stevenson," says Mr Tree, "always seemed to me an epicure in life. He was always intent on extracting the last drop of honey from every flower that came in his way. He was absorbed in the business of the moment, however trivial. As a companion, he was delightfully witty; as a personality, as much a creature of romance as his own creations."

This is simple, and it looks sincere; but it does not touch 'tother side, or hint at, not to say, solve the problem of Stevenson's personality. Had he been the mere Hedonist he could never have done the work he did. Mr Beerbohm Tree certainly did not there see far or all round.

Miss Simpson says:

> "Mr Henley recalls him to Edinburgh folk as he was and as the true Stevenson would have wished to be known—a queer, inexplicable creature, his

Celtic blood showing like a vein of unknown metal in the stolid, steady rock of his sure-founded Stevensonian pedigree. His cousin and model, 'Bob' Stevenson, the art critic, showed that this foreign element came from the men who lit our guiding lights for seamen, not from the gentle-blooded Balfours.

"Mr Henley is right in saying that the gifted boy had not much humour. When the joke was against himself he was very thin-skinned and had a want of balance. This made him feel his honest father's sensible remarks like the sting of a whip."

Miss Simpson then proceeds to say:

"The R. L. Stevenson of old Edinburgh days was a conceited, egotistical youth, but a true and honest one: a youth full of fire and sentiment, protesting he was misunderstood, though he was not. Posing as 'Velvet Coat' among the slums, he did no good to himself. He had not the Dickens aptitude for depicting the ways of life of his adopted friends. When with refined judgment he wanted a figure for a novel, he went back to the Bar he scorned in his callow days and then drew in *Weir of Hermiston*."

CHAPTER V—TRAVELS

His interest in engineering soon went—his mind full of stories and fancies and human nature. As he had told his mother: he did not care about finding what was "the strain on a bridge," he wanted to know something of human beings.

No doubt, much to the disappointment and grief of his father, who wished him as an only son to carry on the traditions of the family, though he had written two engineering essays of utmost promise, the engineering was given up, and he consented to study law. He had already contributed to College Magazines, and had had even a short spell of editing one; of one of these he has given a racy account. Very soon after his call to the Bar articles and essays from his pen began to appear in *Macmillan's*, and later, more regularly in the *Cornhill*. Careful readers soon began to note here the presence of a new force. He had gone on the *Inland Voyage* and an account of it was in hand; and had done that tour in the Cevennes which he has described under the title *Travels with a Donkey in the Cevennes*, with Modestine, sometimes doubting which was the donkey, but on that tour a chill caught either developed a germ of lung disease already present, or produced it; and the results unfortunately remained.

He never practised at the Bar, though he tells facetiously of his one brief. He had chosen his own vocation, which was literature, and the years which followed were, despite the delicacy which showed itself, very busy years. He produced volume on volume. He had written many stories which had never seen the light, but, as he says, passed through the ordeal of the fire by more or less circuitous ways.

By this time some trouble and cause for anxiety had arisen about the lungs, and trials of various places had been made. *Ordered South* suggests the Mediterranean, sunny Italy, the Riviera. Then a sea-trip to America was recommended and undertaken. Unfortunately, he got worse there, his original cause of trouble was complicated with others, and the medical treatment given was stupid, and exaggerated some of the symptoms instead of removing them, All along—up, at all events, to the time of his settlement in Samoa—Stevenson was more or less of an invalid.

Indeed, were I ever to write an essay on the art of wisely "laying-to," as the sailors say, I would point it by a reference to R. L. Stevenson. For there is a wise way of "laying-to" that does not imply inaction, but discreet, well-directed effort, against contrary winds and rough seas, that is, amid obstacles and drawbacks, and even ill-health, where passive and active may balance and give effect to each other. Stevenson was by native instinct and temperament a rover—a lover of adventure, of strange by-ways, errant tracts (as seen in his *Inland Voyage* and *Travels with a Donkey through the Cevennes*—seen yet more, perhaps, in a certain account of a voyage to America as a steerage passenger), lofty mountain-tops, with stronger air, and strange and novel surroundings. He would fain, like Ulysses, be at home in foreign lands, making acquaintance with outlying races, with

> "Cities of men,
> And manners, climates, councils, governments:
> Myself not least, but honoured of them all,
> Far on the ringing plains of windy Troy."

If he could not move about as he would, he would invent, make fancy serve him instead of experience. We thus owe something to the staying and restraining forces in him, and a wise "laying-to"—for his works, which are, in large part, finely-healthy, objective, and in almost everything unlike the work of an invalid, yet, in some degree, were but the devices to beguile the burdens of an invalid's days. Instead of remaining in our climate, it might be, to lie listless and helpless half the day, with no companion but his own thoughts and fancies (not always so pleasant either, if, like Frankenstein's monster, or, better still like the imp in the bottle in the *Arabian Nights*, you cannot, once for all liberate them, and set them adrift on their own charges to visit other people), he made a home in the sweeter air and more steady climate of the South Pacific, where, under the Southern Cross, he could safely and beneficially be as active as he would be involuntarily idle at home, or work only under pressure of hampering conditions. That was surely an illustration of the true "laying-to" with an unaffectedly brave, bright resolution in it.

CHAPTER VI – SOME EARLIER LETTERS

Carlyle was wont to say that, next to a faithful portrait, familiar letters were the best medium to reveal a man. The letters must have been written with no idea of being used for this end, however – free, artless, the unstudied self-revealings of mind and heart. Now, these letters of R. L. Stevenson, written to his friends in England, have a vast value in this way – they reveal the man – reveal him in his strength and his weakness – his ready gift in pleasing and adapting himself to those with whom he corresponded, and his great power at once of adapting himself to his circumstances and of humorously rising superior to them. When he was ill and almost penniless in San Francisco, he could give Mr Colvin this account of his daily routine:

> "Any time between eight and half-past nine in the morning a slender gentleman in an ulster, with a volume buttoned into the breast of it, maybe observed leaving No. 608 Bush and descending Powell with an active step. The gentleman is R. L. Stevenson; the volume relates to Benjamin Franklin, on whom he meditates one of his charming essays. He descends Powell, crosses Market, and descends in Sixth on a branch of the original Pine Street Coffee-House, no less. . . . He seats himself at a table covered with waxcloth, and a pampered menial of High-Dutch extraction, and, indeed, as yet only partially extracted, lays before him a cup of coffee, a roll, and a pat of butter, all, to quote the deity, very good. A while ago, and R. L. Stevenson used to find the supply of butter insufficient; but he has now learned the art to exactitude, and butter and roll expire at the same moment. For this rejection he pays ten cents, or fivepence sterling (#0 0s. 5d.).
>
> "Half an hour later, the inhabitants of Bush Street observed the same slender gentleman armed, like George Washington, with his little hatchet, splitting kindling, and breaking coal for

> his fire. He does this quasi-publicly upon the window-sill; but this is not to be attributed to any love of notoriety, though he is indeed vain of his prowess with the hatchet (which he persists in calling an axe), and daily surprised at the perpetuation of his fingers. The reason is this: That the sill is a strong supporting beam, and that blows of the same emphasis in other parts of his room might knock the entire shanty into hell. Thenceforth, for from three hours, he is engaged darkly with an ink-bottle. Yet he is not blacking his boots, for the only pair that he possesses are innocent of lustre, and wear the natural hue of the material turned up with caked and venerable slush. The youngest child of his landlady remarks several times a day, as this strange occupant enters or quits the house, 'Dere's de author.' Can it be that this bright-haired innocent has found the true clue to the mystery? The being in question is, at least, poor enough to belong to that honourable craft."

Here are a few letters belonging to the winter of 1887-88, nearly all written from Saranac Lake, in the Adirondacks, celebrated by Emerson, and now a most popular holiday resort in the United States, and were originally published in *Scribner's Magazine*. . . "It should be said that, after his long spell of weakness at Bournemouth, Stevenson had gone West in search of health among the bleak hill summits—'on the Canadian border of New York State, very unsettled and primitive and cold.' He had made the voyage in an ocean tramp, the *Ludgate Hill*, the sort of craft which any person not a born child of the sea would shun in horror. Stevenson, however, had 'the finest time conceivable on board the "strange floating menagerie."'" Thus he describes it in a letter to Mr Henry James:

> "Stallions and monkeys and matches made our cargo; and the vast continent of these incongruities rolled the while like a haystack; and the stallions stood hypnotised by the motion, looking through the port at our dinner-table, and winked when the crockery was broken; and the little monkeys stared

> at each other in their cages, and were thrown overboard like little bluish babies; and the big monkey, Jacko, scoured about the ship and rested willingly in my arms, to the ruin of my clothing; and the man of the stallions made a bower of the black tarpaulin, and sat therein at the feet of a raddled divinity, like a picture on a box of chocolates; and the other passengers, when they were not sick, looked on and laughed. Take all this picture, and make it roll till the bell shall sound unexpected notes and the fittings shall break loose in our stateroom, and you have the voyage of the *Ludgate Hill*. She arrived in the port of New York without beer, porter, soda-water, curagoa, fresh meat, or fresh water; and yet we lived, and we regret her."

He discovered this that there is no joy in the Universe comparable to life on a villainous ocean tramp, rolling through a horrible sea in company with a cargo of cattle.

> "I have got one good thing of my sea voyage; it is proved the sea agrees heartily with me, and my mother likes it; so if I get any better, or no worse, my mother will likely hire a yacht for a month or so in the summer. Good Lord! what fun! Wealth is only useful for two things: a yacht and a string quartette. For these two I will sell my soul. Except for these I hold that #700 a year is as much as anybody can possibly want; and I have had more, so I know, for the extra coins were of no use, excepting for illness, which damns everything. I was so happy on board that ship, I could not have believed it possible; we had the beastliest weather, and many discomforts; but the mere fact of its being a tramp ship gave us many comforts. We could cut about with the men and officers, stay in the wheel-house, discuss all manner of things, and really be a little at sea. And truly there is nothing else. I had literally forgotten what happiness was, and the full mind—full of external and physical things, not full

of cares and labours, and rot about a fellow's behaviour. My heart literally sang; I truly care for nothing so much as for that.

"To go ashore for your letters and hang about the pier among the holiday yachtsmen—that's fame, that's glory—and nobody can take it away."

At Saranac Lake the Stevensons lived in a "wind-beleaguered hill-top hat-box of a house," which suited the invalid, but, on the other hand, invalided his wife. Soon after getting there he plunged into *The Master of Ballantrae*.

"No thought have I now apart from it, and I have got along up to page ninety-two of the draught with great interest. It is to me a most seizing tale: there are some fantastic elements, the most is a dead genuine human problem—human tragedy, I should say rather. It will be about as long, I imagine, as *Kidnapped*. . . . I have done most of the big work, the quarrel, duel between the brothers, and the announcement of the death to Clementina and my Lord—Clementina, Henry, and Mackellar (nicknamed Squaretoes) are really very fine fellows; the Master is all I know of the devil; I have known hints of him, in the world, but always cowards: he is as bold as a lion, but with the same deadly, causeless duplicity I have watched with so much surprise in my two cowards. 'Tis true, I saw a hint of the same nature in another man who was not a coward; but he had other things to attend to; the Master has nothing else but his devilry."

His wife grows seriously ill, and Stevenson has to turn to household work.

"Lloyd and I get breakfast; I have now, 10.15, just got the dishes washed and the kitchen all clean, and sit down to give you as much news as I have spirit for, after such an engagement. Glass is a thing that really breaks my spirit; and I do not

> like to fail, and with glass I cannot reach the work of my high calling—the artist's."

In the midst of such domestic tasks and entanglements he writes *The Master*, and very characteristically gets dissatisfied with the last parts, "which shame, perhaps degrade, the beginning."

Of Mr Kipling this is his judgment—in the year 1890:

> "Kipling is by far the most promising young man who has appeared since—ahem—I appeared. He amazes me by his precocity and various endowments. But he alarms me by his copiousness and haste. He should shield his fire with both hands, 'and draw up all his strength and sweetness in one ball.' ('Draw all his strength and all his sweetness up into one ball'? I cannot remember Marvell's words.) So the critics have been saying to me; but I was never capable of—and surely never guilty of—such a debauch of production. At this rate his works will soon fill the habitable globe, and surely he was armed for better conflicts than these succinct sketches and flying leaves of verse? I look on, I admire, I rejoice for myself; but in a kind of ambition we all have for our tongue and literature I am wounded. If I had this man's fertility and courage, it seems to me I could heave a pyramid.
>
> "Well, we begin to be the old fogies now, and it was high time *something* rose to take our places. Certainly Kipling has the gifts; the fairy godmothers were all tipsy at his christening. What will he do with them?"

Of the rest of Stevenson's career we cannot speak at length, nor is it needful. How in steady succession came his triumphs: came, too, his trials from ill-health—how he spent winters at Davos Platz, Bournemouth, and tried other places in America; and how, at last, good fortune led him to the South Pacific. After many voyagings and wanderings among the islands, he settled near Apia, in Samoa, early in 1890, cleared some four hundred acres, and built a house; where, while he wrote what delighted the English-speaking race, he took on himself the defence of the natives against foreign interlopers, writing under the title *A Footnote to History*, the most powerful *exposi* of the mischief they had done and were doing there. He was the beloved of the natives, as he made himself the friend of all with whom he came in contact. There, as at home, he worked—worked with the same determination and in the enjoyment of better health. The obtaining idea with him, up to the end, as it had been from early life, was a brave, resolute, cheerful endeavour to make the best of it.

"I chose Samoa instead of Honolulu," he told Mr W. H. Trigg, who reports the talk in *Cassells' Magazine*, "for the simple and eminently satisfactory reason that it is less civilised. Can you not conceive that it is awful fun?" His house was called "Vailima," which means Five Waters in the Samoan, and indicates the number of streams that flow by the spot.

CHAPTER VII – THE VAILIMA LETTERS

The Vailima Letters, written to Mr Sidney Colvin and other friends, are in their way delightful if not inimitable: and this, in spite of the idea having occurred to him, that some use might hereafter be made of these letters for publication purposes. There is, indeed, as little trace of any change in the style through this as well could be – the utterly familiar, easy, almost child-like flow remains, unmarred by self-consciousness or tendency "to put it on."

In June, 1892, Stevenson says:

> "It came over me the other day suddenly that this diary of mine to you would make good pickings after I am dead, and a man could make some kind of a book out of it, without much trouble. So for God's sake don't lose them, and they will prove a piece of provision for 'my floor old family,' as Simeli calls it."

But their great charm remains: they are as free and gracious and serious and playful and informal as before. Stevenson's traits of character are all here: his largeness of heart, his delicacy, his sympathy, his fun, his pathos, his boylike frolicsomeness, his fine courage, his love of the sea (for he was by nature a sailor), his passion for action and adventure despite his ill-health, his great patience with others and fine adaptability to their temper (he says that he never gets out of temper with those he has to do with), his unbounded, big-hearted hopefulness, and fine perseverance in face of difficulties. What could be better than the way in which he tells that in January, 1892, when he had a bout of influenza and was dictating *St Ives* to his stepdaughter, Mrs Strong, he was "reduced to dictating to her in the deaf-and-dumb alphabet"? – and goes on:

> "The amanuensis has her head quite turned, and believes herself to be the author of this novel [*and is to some extent.* – A.M.] and as the creature (!) has not been wholly useless in the matter [*I told you so!* – A.M.] I propose to foster her vanity by a little commemoration gift! . . . I shall tell you on some

> other occasion, and when the A.M. is out of hearing, how *very* much I propose to invest in this testimonial; but I may as well inform you at once that I intend it to be cheap, sir—damned cheap! My idea of running amanuenses is by praise, not pudding, flattery, and not coins."

Truly, a rare and rich nature which could thus draw sunshine out of its trials!—which, by aid of the true philosopher's stone of cheerfulness and courage, could transmute the heavy dust and clay to gold.

His interests are so wide that he is sometimes pulled in different and conflicting directions, as in the contest between his desire to aid Mataafa and the other chiefs, and his literary work—between letters to the *Times* about Samoan politics, and, say, *David Balfour*. Here is a characteristic bit in that strain:

> "I have a good dose of the devil in my pipestem atomy; I have had my little holiday outing in my kick at *The Young Chevalier*, and I guess I can settle to *David Balfour*, to-morrow or Friday like a little man. I wonder if any one had ever more energy upon so little strength? I know there is a frost; . . . but I mean to break that frost inside two years, and pull off a big success, and Vanity whispers in my ear that I have the strength. If I haven't, whistle owre the lave o't! I can do without glory, and perhaps the time is not far off when I can do without corn. It is a time coming soon enough, anyway; and I have endured some two and forty years without public shame, and had a good time as I did it. If only I could secure a violent death, what a fine success! I wish to die in my boots; no more Land of Counterpane for me. To be drowned, to be shot, to be thrown from a horse—ay, to be hanged, rather than pass again through that slow dissolution."

He would not consent to act the invalid unless the spring ran down altogether; was keen for exercise and for mixing among men—his native servants if no others were near by. Here is a bit of confession and casuistry quite ` *la* Stevenson:

> "To come down covered with mud and drenched with sweat and rain after some hours in the bush, change, rub down, and take a chair in the verandah, is to taste a quiet conscience. And the strange thing that I mark is this: If I go out and make sixpence, bossing my labourers and plying the cutlass or the spade, idiot conscience applauds me; if I sit in the house and make twenty pounds, idiot conscience wails over my neglect and the day wasted."

His relish for companionship is indeed strong. At one place he says:

> "God knows I don't care who I chum with perhaps I like sailors best, but to go round and sue and sneak to keep a crowd together—never!"

If Stevenson's natural bent was to be an explorer, a mountain-climber, or a sailor—to sail wide seas, or to range on mountain-tops to gain free and extensive views—yet he inclines well to farmer work, and indeed, has to confess it has a rare attraction for him.

> "I went crazy over outdoor work," he says at one place, "and had at last to confine myself to the house, or literature must have gone by the board. *Nothing* is so interesting as weeding, clearing, and path-making: the oversight of labourers becomes a disease. It is quite an effort not to drop into the farmer; and it does make you feel so well."

The odd ways of these Samoans, their pride of position, their vices, their virtues, their vanities, their small thefts, their tricks, their delightful *insouciance* sometimes, all amused him. He found in them a fine field of study and observation—a source of fun and fund of humanity—as this bit about the theft of some piglings will sufficiently prove:

> "Last night three piglings were stolen from one of our pig-pens. The great Lafaele appeared to my

wife uneasy, so she engaged him in conversation on the subject, and played upon him the following engaging trick: You advance your two forefingers towards the sitter's eyes; he closes them, whereupon you substitute (on his eyelids) the fore and middle fingers of the left hand, and with your right (which he supposes engaged) you tap him on the head and back. When you let him open his eyes, he sees you withdrawing the two forefingers. 'What that?' asked Lafaele. 'My devil,' says Fanny. 'I wake um, my devil. All right now. He go catch the man that catch my pig.' About an hour afterwards Lafaele came for further particulars. 'Oh, all right,' my wife says. 'By-and-by that man be sleep, devil go sleep same place. By-and-by that man plenty sick. I no care. What for he take my pig?' Lafaele cares plenty; I don't think he is the man, though he may be; but he knows him, and most likely will eat some of that pig to-night. He will not eat with relish.'"

Yet in spite of this R. L. Stevenson declares that:

> "They are a perfectly honest people: nothing of value has ever been taken from our house, where doors and windows are always wide open; and upon one occasion when white ants attacked the silver chest, the whole of my family treasure lay spread upon the floor of the hall for two days unguarded."

Here is a bit on a work of peace, a reflection on a day's weeding at Vailima—in its way almost as touching as any:

> "I wonder if any one had ever the same attitude to Nature as I hold, and have held for so long? This business fascinates me like a tune or a passion; yet all the while I thrill with a strong distaste. The horror of the thing, objective and subjective, is always present to my mind; the horror of creeping things, a superstitious horror of the void and the powers

> about me, the horror of my own devastation and continual murders. The life of the plants comes through my finger-tips, their struggles go to my heart like supplications. I feel myself blood-boltered; then I look back on my cleared grass, and count myself an ally in a fair quarrel, and make stout my heart."

Here, again, is the way in which he celebrates an act of friendly kindness on the part of Mr Gosse:

> "My dear Gosse,—Your letter was to me such a bright spot that I answer it right away to the prejudice of other correspondents or—dants (don't know how to spell it) who have prior claims. . . . It is the history of our kindnesses that alone makes this world tolerable. If it were not for that, for the effect of kind words, kind looks, kind letters, multiplying, spreading, making one happy through another and bringing forth benefits, some thirty, some fifty, some a thousandfold, I should be tempted to think our life a practical jest in the worst possible spirit. So your four pages have confirmed my philosophy as well as consoled my heart in these ill hours."

CHAPTER VIII – WORK OF LATER YEARS

Mr Hammerton, in his *Stevensoniana* (pp. 323-4), has given the humorous inscriptions on the volumes of his works which Stevenson presented to Dr Trudeau, who attended him when he was in Saranac in 1887-88 – very characteristic in every way, and showing fully Stevenson's fine appreciation of any attention or service. On the *Dr Jekyll and Mr Hyde* volume he wrote:

> "Trudeau was all the winter at my side:
> I never saw the nose of Mr Hyde."

And on *Kidnapped* is this:

> "Here is the one sound page of all my writing,
> The one I'm proud of and that I delight in."

Stevenson was exquisite in this class of efforts, and were they all collected they would form indeed, a fine supplement and illustration of the leading lesson of his essays – the true art of pleasing others, and of truly pleasing one's self at the same time. To my thinking the finest of all in this line is the legal (?) deed by which he conveyed his birthday to little Miss Annie Ide, the daughter of Mr H. C. Ide, a well-known American, who was for several years a resident of Upolo, in Samoa, first as Land Commissioner, and later as Chief Justice under the joint appointment of England, Germany, and the United States. While living at Apia, Mr Ide and his family were very intimate with the family of R. L. Stevenson. Little Annie was a special pet and protigi of Stevenson and his wife. After the return of the Ides to their American home, Stevenson "deeded" to Annie his birthday in the following unique document:

> I, Robert Louis Stevenson, advocate of the Scots Bar, author of *The Master of Ballantrae* and *Moral Emblems*, civil engineer, sole owner and patentee of the palace and plantation known as Vailima, in the island of Upolo, Samoa, a British subject, being in sound mind, and pretty well, I thank you, in mind and body;

In consideration that Miss Annie H. Ide, daughter of H. C. Ide, in the town of Saint Johnsbury, in the County of Caledonia, in the State of Vermont, United States of America, was born, out of all reason, upon Christmas Day, and is, therefore, out of all justice, denied the consolation and profit of a proper birthday;

And considering that I, the said Robert Louis Stevenson, have attained the age when we never mention it, and that I have now no further use for a birthday of any description;

And in consideration that I have met H. C. Ide, the father of the said Annie H. Ide, and found him as white a land commissioner as I require, I have transferred, and do hereby transfer, to the said Annie H. Ide, all and whole of my rights and privileges in the 13th day of November, formerly my birthday, now, hereby and henceforth, the birthday of the said Annie H. Ide, to have, hold, exercise, and enjoy the same in the customary manner, by the sporting of fine raiment, eating of rich meats, and receipt of gifts, compliments, and copies of verse, according to the manner of our ancestors;

And I direct the said Annie H. Ide to add to the said name of Annie H. Ide the name of Louisa—at least in private—and I charge her to use my said birthday with moderation and humanity, *et tamquam bona filia familias*, the said birthday not being so young as it once was and having carried me in a very satisfactory manner since I can remember;

And in case the said Annie H. Ide shall neglect or contravene either of the above conditions, I hereby revoke the donation and transfer my rights in the said birthday to the President of the United States of America for the time being.

In witness whereof I have hereto set my hand and seal this 19th day of June, in the year of grace eighteen hundred and ninety-one.

Robert Louis Stevenson. [Seal.]

Witness, Lloyd Osbourne.

Witness, Harold Watts.

He died in Samoa in December 1894—not from phthisis or anything directly connected with it, but from the bursting of a blood-vessel and suffusion of blood on the brain. He had up to the moment almost of his sudden and unexpected death been busy on *Weir of Hermiston* and *St Ives*, which he left unfinished—the latter having been brought to a conclusion by Mr Quiller-Couch.

CHAPTER IX – SOME CHARACTERISTICS

In Stevenson we lost one of the most powerful writers of our day, as well as the most varied in theme and style. When I use the word "powerful," I do not mean merely the producing of the most striking or sensational results, nor the facility of weaving a fascinating or blood-curdling plot; I mean the writer who seemed always to have most in reserve – a secret fund of power and fascination which always pointed beyond the printed page, and set before the attentive and careful reader a strange but fascinating *personality*. Other authors have done that in measure. There was Hawthorne, behind whose writings there is always the wistful, cold, far-withdrawn spectator of human nature – eerie, inquisitive, and, I had almost said, inquisitorial – a little bloodless, eerie, weird, and cobwebby. There was Dr Wendell Holmes, with his problems of heredity, of race-mixture and weird inoculation, as in *Elsie Venner* and *The Guardian Angel*, and there were Poe and Charles Whitehead. Stevenson, in a few of his writings – in one of the *Merry Men* chapters and in *Dr Jekyll and Mr Hyde*, and, to some extent, in *The Master of Ballantrae* – showed that he could enter on the obscure and, in a sense, weird and metaphysical elements in human life; though always there was, too, a touch at least of gloomy suggestion, from which, as it seemed, he could not there wholly escape. But always, too, there was a touch that suggests the universal.

Even in the stories that would be classed as those of incident and adventure merely, *Treasure Island*, *Kidnapped*, and the rest, there is a sense as of some unaffected but fine symbolism that somehow touches something of possibility in yourself as you read. The simplest narrative from his hand proclaimed itself a deep study in human nature – its motives tendencies, and possibilities. In these stories there is promise at once of the most realistic imagination, the most fantastic romance, keen insights into some sides of human nature, and weird fancies, as well as the most delicate and dainty pictures of character. And this is precisely what we have – always with a vein of the finest autobiography – a kind of select and indirect self-revelation – often with a touch of quaintness, a subdued humour, and sweet-blooded vagary, if we may be allowed the word, which make you feel towards the writer as towards a friend.

He was too much an artist to overdo this, and his strength lies there, that generally he suggests and turns away at the right point, with a smile, as you ask for *more*. Look how he sets, half slyly, these words into the mouth of David Balfour on his first meeting with Catriona in one of the steep wynds or closes off the High Street of Edinburgh:

> "There is no greater wonder than the way the face of a young woman fits in a man's mind, and stays there, and he never could tell you why: it just seems it was the thing he wanted."

Take this alongside of his remark made to his mother while still a youth—"that he did not care to understand the strain on a bridge" (when he tried to study engineering); what he wanted was something with human nature in it. His style, in his essays, etc., where he writes in his own person, is most polished, full of phrases finely drawn; when he speaks through others, as in *Kidnapped* and *David Balfour*, it is still fine and effective, and generally it is fairly true to the character, with cunning glimpses, nevertheless, of his own temper and feeling too. He makes us feel his confidants and friends, as has been said. One could almost construct a biography from his essays and his novels—the one would give us the facts of his life suffused with fancy and ideal colour, humour and fine observation not wanting; the other would give us the history of his mental and moral being and development, and of the traits and determinations which he drew from along a lengthened line of progenitors. How characteristic it is of him—a man who for so many years suffered as an invalid—that he should lay it down that the two great virtues, including all others, were cheerfulness and delight in labour.

One writer has very well said on this feature in Stevenson:

> "Other authors have struggled bravely against physical weakness, but their work has not usually been of a creative order, dependent for its success on high animal spirits. They have written histories, essays, contemplative or didactic poems, works which may more or less be regarded as 'dull narcotics numbing pain.' But who, in so fragile a frame as Robert Louis Stevenson's, has retained such indomitable elasticity, such fertility of inven-

> tion, such unflagging energy, not merely to collect and arrange, but to project and body forth? Has any true 'maker' been such an incessant sufferer? From his childhood, as he himself said apropos of the *Child's Garden*, he could 'speak with less authority of gardens than of that other "land of counterpane."' There were, indeed, a few years of adolescence during which his health was tolerable, but they were years of apprenticeship to life and art ('pioching,' as he called it), not of serious production. Though he was a precocious child, his genius ripened slowly, and it was just reaching maturity when the 'wolverine,' as he called his disease, fixed its fangs in his flesh. From that time forward not only did he live with death at his elbow in an almost literal sense (he used to carry his left arm in a sling lest a too sudden movement should bring on a hfmorrhage), but he had ever-recurring intervals of weeks and months during which he was totally unfit for work; while even at the best of times he had to husband his strength most jealously. Add to all this that he was a slow and laborious writer, who would take more pains with a phrase than Scott with a chapter—then look at the stately shelf of his works, brimful of impulse, initiative, and the joy of life, and say whether it be an exaggeration to call his tenacity and fortitude unique!"

Samoa, with its fine climate, prolonged his life—we had fain hoped that in that air he found so favourable he might have lived for many years, to add to the precious stock of innocent delight he has given to the world—to do yet more and greater. It was not to be. They buried him, with full native honours as to a chief, on the top of Vaea mountain, 1300 feet high—a road for the coffin to pass being cut through the woods on the slopes of the hill. There he has a resting-place not all unfit—for he sought the pure and clearer air on the heights from whence there are widest prospects; yet not in the spot he would have chosen—for his heart was at home, and not very long before his death he sang, surely with pathetic reference now:

"Spring shall come, come again, calling up the moorfowl,
Spring shall bring the sun and rain, bring the bees and flowers,
Red shall the heather bloom over hill and valley,
Soft flow the stream thro' the even-flowing hours;
Fair the day shine, as it shone upon my childhood –
Fair shine the day on the house with open door;
Birds come and cry there, and twitter in the chimney –
But I go for ever and come again no more."

CHAPTER X – A SAMOAN MEMORIAL OF R. L. STEVENSON

A few weeks after his death, the mail from Samoa, brought to Stevenson's friends, myself among the number, a precious, if pathetic, memorial of the master. It is in the form of "A Letter to Mr Stevenson's Friends," by his stepson, Mr Lloyd Osbourne, and bears the motto from Walt Whitman, "I have been waiting for you these many years. Give me your hand and welcome." Mr Osbourne gives a full account of the last hours.

> "He wrote hard all that morning of the last day; his half-finished book, *Hermiston,* he judged the best he had ever written, and the sense of successful effort made him buoyant and happy as nothing else could. In the afternoon the mail fell to be answered – not business correspondence, for this was left till later – but replies to the long, kindly letters of distant friends received but two days since, and still bright in memory. At sunset he came downstairs; rallied his wife about the forebodings she could not shake off; talked of a lecturing tour to America that he was eager to make, 'as he was now so well'; and played a game of cards with her to drive away her melancholy. He said he was hungry; begged her assistance to help him make a salad for the evening meal; and, to enhance the little feast he brought up a bottle of old Burgundy from the cellar. He was helping his wife on the verandah, and gaily talking, when suddenly he put both hands to his head and cried out, 'What's that?' Then he asked quickly, 'Do I look strange?' Even as he did so he fell on his knees beside her. He was helped into the great hall, between his wife and his body-servant, Sosimo, losing consciousness instantly as he lay back in the armchair that had once been his grandfather's. Little time was lost in bringing the doctors – Anderson of the man-

of-war, and his friend, Dr Funk. They looked at him and shook their heads; they laboured strenuously, and left nothing undone. But he had passed the bounds of human skill. He had grown so well and strong, that his wasted lungs were unable to bear the stress of returning health."

Then 'tis told how the Rev. Mr Clarke came and prayed by him; and how, soon after, the chiefs were summoned, and came, bringing their fine mats, which, laid on the body, almost hid the Union jack in which it had been wrapped. One of the old Mataafa chiefs, who had been in prison, and who had been one of those who worked on the making of the "Road of the Loving Heart" (the road of gratitude which the chiefs had made up to Mr Stevenson's house as a mark of their appreciation of his efforts on their behalf), came and crouched beside the body and said:

> "I am only a poor Samoan, and ignorant. Others are rich, and can give Tusitala [6] the parting presents of rich, fine mats; I am poor, and can give nothing this last day he receives his friends. Yet I am not afraid to come and look the last time in my friend's face, never to see him more till we meet with God. Behold! Tusitala is dead; Mataafa is also dead. These two great friends have been taken by God. When Mataafa was taken, who was our support but Tusitala? We were in prison, and he cared for us. We were sick, and he made us well. We were hungry, and he fed us. The day was no longer than his kindness. You are great people, and full of love. Yet who among you is so great as Tusitala? What is your love to his love? Our clan was Mataafa's clan, for whom I speak this day; therein was Tusitala also. We mourn them both."

A select company of Samoans would not be deterred, and watched by the body all night, chanting songs, with bits of Catholic prayers; and in the morning the work began of clearing a path through the wood on the hill to the spot on the crown where Mr Stevenson had expressed a wish to be buried. The following prayer, which Mr Stevenson had written and read aloud to his family only the night before, was read by Mr Clarke in the service:

> "We beseech thee, Lord, to behold us with favour, folk of many families and nations, gathered together in the peace of this roof; weak men and women, subsisting under the covert of Thy patience. Be patient still; suffer us yet a while longer—with our broken purposes of good, with our idle endeavours against evil—suffer us a while longer to endure, and (if it may be) help us to do better. Bless to us our extraordinary mercies; if the day come when these must be taken, have us play the man under affliction. Be with our friends; be with ourselves. Go with each of us to rest: if any awake, temper to them the dark hours of watching; and when the day returns to us, our Sun and Comforter, call us up with morning faces and with morning hearts—eager to labour—eager to be happy, if happiness shall be our portion; and if the day be marked for sorrow, strong to endure it.
>
> "We thank Thee and praise Thee, and in the words of Him to whom this day is sacred, close our oblations."

Mr Bazzet M. Haggard, H.B.M., Land-Commissioner, tells, by way of reminiscence, the story of "The Road of Good Heart," how it came to be built, and of the great feast Mr Stevenson gave at the close of the work, at which, in the course of his speech, he said:

> "You are all aware in some degree of what has happened. You know those chiefs to have been prisoners; you perhaps know that during the term of their confinement I had it in my power to do them certain favours. One thing some of you cannot know, that they were immediately repaid by answering attentions. They were liberated by the new Administration. . . . As soon as they were free men—owing no man anything—instead of going home to their own places and families, they came

to me. They offered to do this work (to make this road) for me as a free gift, without hire, without supplies, and I was tempted at first to refuse their offer. I knew the country to be poor; I knew famine threatening; I knew their families long disorganised for want of supervision. Yet I accepted, because I thought the lesson of that road might be more useful to Samoa than a thousand bread-fruit trees, and because to myself it was an exquisite pleasure to receive that which was so handsomely offered. It is now done; you have trod it to-day in coming hither. It has been made for me by chiefs; some of them old, some sick, all newly delivered from a harassing confinement, and in spite of weather unusually hot and insalubrious. I have seen these chiefs labour valiantly with their own hands upon the work, and I have set up over it, now that it is finished the name of 'The Road of Gratitude' (the road of loving hearts), and the names of those that built it. 'In perpetuam memoriam,' we say, and speak idly. At least, as long as my own life shall be spared it shall be here perpetuated; partly for my pleasure and in my gratitude; partly for others continually to publish the lesson of this road."

And turning to the chiefs, Mr Stevenson said:

"I will tell you, chiefs, that when I saw you working on that road, my heart grew warm; not with gratitude only, but with hope. It seemed to me that I read the promise of something good for Samoa; it seemed to me as I looked at you that you were a company of warriors in a battle, fighting for the defence of our common country against all aggression. For there is a time to fight and a time to dig. You Samoans may fight, you may conquer twenty times, and thirty times, and all will be in vain. There is but one way to defend Samoa. Hear it, before it is too late. It is to make roads and gardens, and care for your trees, and sell their produce wisely; and, in one word, to occupy and use your country. If you do not, others will. . . .

"I love Samoa and her people. I love the land. I have chosen it to be my home while I live, and my grave after I am dead, and I love the people, and have chosen them to be my people, to live and die with. And I see that the day is come now of the great battle; of the great and the last opportunity by which it shall be decided whether you are to pass away like those other races of which I have been speaking, or to stand fast and have your children living on and honouring your memory in the land you received of your fathers."

Mr James H. Mulligan, U.S. Consul, told of the feast of Thanksgiving Day on the 29th November prior to Mr Stevenson's death, and how at great pains he had procured for it the necessary turkey, and how Mrs Stevenson had found a fair substitute for the pudding. In the course of his speech in reply to an unexpected proposal of "The Host," Mr Stevenson said:

"There on my right sits she who has but lately from our own loved native land come back to me—she to whom, with no lessening of affection to those others to whom I cling, I love better than all the world besides—my mother. From the opposite end of the table, my wife, who has been all in all to me, when the days were very dark, looks tonight into my eyes—while we have both grown a bit older—with undiminished and undiminishing affection.

"Childless, yet on either side of me sits that good woman, my daughter, and the stalwart man, my son, and both have been and are more than son and daughter to me, and have brought into my life mirth and beauty. Nor is this all. There sits the bright boy dear to my heart, full of the flow and the spirits of boyhood, so that I can even know that for a time at least we have still the voice of a child in the house."

Mr A. W. Mackay gives an account of the funeral and a description of the burial-place, ending:

> "Tofa Tusitala! Sleep peacefully! on thy mountain-top, alone in Nature's sanctity, where the wooddove's note, the moaning of the waves as they break unceasingly on the distant reef, and the sighing of the winds in the distant tavai trees chant their requiem."

The Rev. Mr Clarke tells of the constant and active interest Mr Stevenson took in the missionaries and their work, often aiding them by his advice and fine insight into the character of the natives; and a translation follows of a dirge by one of the chiefs, so fine that we must give it:

I.

"Listen, O this world, as I tell of the disaster
That befell in the late afternoon;
That broke like a wave of the sea
Suddenly and swiftly, blinding our eyes.
Alas for Loia who speaks tears in his voice!

Refrain—Groan and weep, O my heart, in its sorrow.
Alas for Tusitala, who rests in the forest!
Aimlessly we wait, and sorrowing. Will he again return?
Lament, O Vailima, waiting and ever waiting!
Let us search and inquire of the captain of ships,
'Be not angry, but has not Tusitala come?'

II.

"Teuila, sorrowing one, come thou hither!
Prepare me a letter, and I will carry it.
Let her Majesty Victoria be told
That Tusitala, the loving one, has been taken hence.

Refrain—Groan and weep, O my heart, etc., etc.

III.

"Alas! my heart weeps with anxious grief
As I think of the days before us:
Of the white men gathering for the Christmas assembly!
Alas for Aolele! left in her loneliness,
And the men of Vailima, who weep together
Their leader—their leader being taken.

Refrain—Groan and weep, O my heart, etc., etc.

IV.

"Alas! O my heart! it weeps unceasingly
When I think of his illness
Coming upon him with fatal swiftness.
Would that it waited a glance or a word from him,
Or some token, some token from us of our love.

Refrain—Groan and weep, O my heart, etc., etc.

V.

"Grieve, O my heart! I cannot bear to look on
All the chiefs who are there now assembling:
Alas, Tusitala! Thou art not here!
I look hither and thither in vain for thee.

Refrain—Groan and weep, O my heart, etc., etc."

And the little booklet closes with Mr Stevenson's own lines:

"REQUIEM.

Under the wide and starry sky,
Dig the grave and let me lie;
Glad did I live and gladly die,
And I laid me down with a will.
This be the verse you grave for me:
'Here he lies where he longed to be;
Home is the sailor, home from sea;
And the hunter home from the hill.'"

Every touch tells here was a man, with heart and head, with soul and mind intent on the loftiest things; simple, great,

> "Like one of the simple great ones gone
> For ever and ever by.

His character towered after all far above his books; great and beautiful though they were. Ready for friendship; from all meanness free. So, too, the Samoans felt. This, surely, was what Goethe meant when he wrote:

> "The clear head and stout heart,
> However far they roam,
> Yet in every truth have part,
> Are everywhere at home."

His manliness, his width of sympathy, his practicality, his range of interests were in nothing more seen than in his contributions to the history of Samoa, as specially exhibited in *A Footnote to History* and his letters to the *Times*. He was, on this side, in no sense a dreamer, but a man of acute observation and quick eye for passing events and the characters that were in them with sympathy equal to his discernments. His portraits of certain Germans and others in these writings, and his power of tracing effects to remote and underlying causes, show sufficiently what he might have done in the field of history, had not higher voices called him. His adaptation to the life in Samoa, and his assumption of the semi-patriarchal character in his own sphere there, were only tokens of the presence of the same traits as have just been dwelt on.

CHAPTER XI – MISS STUBBS' RECORD OF A PILGRIMAGE

Mrs Strong, in her chapter of *Table Talk in Memories of Vailima,* tells a story of the natives' love for Stevenson. "The other day the cook was away," she writes, "and Louis, who was busy writing, took his meals in his room. Knowing there was no one to cook his lunch, he told Sosimo to bring him some bread and cheese. To his surprise he was served with an excellent meal – an omelette, a good salad, and perfect coffee. 'Who cooked this?' asked Louis in Samoan. 'I did,' said Sosimo. 'Well,' said Louis, 'great is your wisdom.' Sosimo bowed and corrected him – 'Great is my love!'"

Miss Stubbs, in her *Stevenson's Shrine; the Record of a Pilgrimage,* illustrates the same devotion. On the top of Mount Vaea, she writes, is the massive sarcophagus, "not an ideal structure by any means, not even beautiful, and yet in its massive ruggedness it somehow suited the man and the place."

"The wind sighed softly in the branches of the 'Tavau' trees, from out the green recesses of the 'Toi' came the plaintive coo of the wood-pigeon. In and out of the branches of the magnificent 'Fau' tree, which overhangs the grave, a king-fisher, sea-blue, iridescent, flitted to and fro, whilst a scarlet hibiscus, in full flower, showed up royally against the gray lichened cement. All around was light and life and colour, and I said to myself, 'He is made one with nature'; he is now, body and soul and spirit, commingled with the loveliness around. He who longed in life to scale the height, he who attained his wish only in death, has become in himself a parable of fulfilment. No need now for that heart-sick cry: –

> "'Sing me a song of a lad that is gone,
> Say, could that lad be I?'

No need now for the despairing finality of:

> "'I have trod the upward and the downward slope,
> I have endured and done in the days of yore,
> I have longed for all, and bid farewell to hope,
> And I have lived, and loved, and closed the door.'

> "Death has set his seal of peace on the unequal conflict of mind and matter; the All-Mother has gathered him to herself.
>
> "In years to come, when his grave is perchance forgotten, a rugged ruin, home of the lizard and the bat, Tusitala—the story-teller—'the man with a heart of gold' (as I so often heard him designated in the Islands), will live, when it may be his tales have ceased to interest, in the tender remembrance of those whose lives he beautified, and whose hearts he warmed into gratitude."

The chiefs have prohibited the use of firearms or other weapons on Mount Vaea, "in order that the birds may live there undisturbed and unafraid, and build their nests in the trees around Tusitala's grave."

Miss Stubbs has many records of the impression produced on those he came in contact with in Samoa—white men and women as well as natives. She met a certain Austrian Count, who adored Stevenson's memory. Over his camp bed was a framed photograph of R. L. Stevenson.

> "So," he said, "I keep him there, for he was my saviour, and I wish 'good-night' and 'good-morning,' every day, both to himself and to his old home." The Count then told us that when he was stopping at Vailima he used to have his bath daily on the verandah below his room. One lovely morning he got up very early, got into the bath, and splashed and sang, feeling very well and very happy, and at last beginning to sing very loudly, he forgot Mr Stevenson altogether. All at once there was Stevenson himself, his hair all ruffled up, his eyes full of anger. "Man," he said, "you and your infernal row have cost me more than two hundred pounds in ideas," and with that he was gone, but he did not address the Count again the whole of that day. Next morning he had forgotten

> the Count's offence and was just as friendly as ever, but—the noise was never repeated!

Another of the Count's stories greatly amused the visitors:

> "An English lord came all the way to Samoa in his yacht to see Mr Stevenson, and found him in his cool Kimino sitting with the ladies, and drinking tea on his verandah; the whole party had their feet bare. The English lord thought that he must have called at the wrong time, and offered to go away, but Mr Stevenson called out to him, and brought him back, and made him stay to dinner. They all went away to dress, and the guest was left sitting alone in the verandah. Soon they came back, Mr Osbourne and Mr Stevenson wearing the form of dress most usual in that hot climate a white mess jacket, and white trousers, but their feet were still bare. The guest put up his eyeglass and stared for a bit, then he looked down upon his own beautifully shod feet, and sighed. They all talked and laughed until the ladies came in, the ladies in silk dresses, befrilled with lace, but still with bare feet, and the guest took a covert look through his eyeglass and gasped, but when he noticed that there were gold bangles on Mrs Strong's ankles and rings upon her toes, he could bear no more and dropped his eyeglass on the ground of the verandah breaking it all to bits."

Miss Stubbs met on the other side of the island a photographer who told her this:

> "I had but recently come to Samoa," he said, "and was standing one day in my shop when Mr Stevenson came in and spoke. 'Man,' he said, 'I tak ye to be a Scotsman like mysel'.'
>
> "I would I could have claimed a kinship," deplored the photographer, "but, alas! I am English to the backbone, with never a drop of Scotch blood

> in my veins, and I told him this, regretting the absence of the blood tie."
>
> "'I could have sworn your back was the back of a Scotsman,' was his comment, 'but,' and he held out his hand, 'you look sick, and there is a fellowship in sickness not to be denied.' I said I was not strong, and had come to the Island on account of my health. 'Well, then,' replied Mr Stevenson, 'it shall be my business to help you to get well; come to Vailima whenever you like, and if I am out, ask for refreshment, and wait until I come in, you will always find a welcome there.'"
>
> At this point my informant turned away, and there was a break in his voice as he exclaimed, "Ah, the years go on, and I don't miss him less, but more; next to my mother he was the best friend I ever had: a man with a heart of gold; his house was a second home to me."

Stevenson's experience shows how easy it is with a certain type of man, to restore the old feudal conditions of service and relationship. Stevenson did this in essentials in Samoa. He tells us how he managed to get good service out of the Samoans (who are accredited with great unwillingness to work); and this he *did* by firm, but generous, kindly, almost brotherly treatment, reviving, as it were, a kind of clan life—giving a livery of certain colours—symbol of all this. A little fellow of eight, he tells, had been taken into the household, made a pet of by Mrs Strong, his stepdaughter, and had had a dress given to him, like that of the men; and, when one day he had strolled down by himself as far as the hotel, and the master of it, seeing him, called out in Samoan, "Hi, youngster, who are you?" The eight-year-old replied, "Why, don't you see for yourself? I am one of the Vailima men!"

The story of the *Road of the Loving Heart* was but another fine attestation of it.

CHAPTER XII – HIS GENIUS AND METHODS

To have created a school of idolaters, who will out and out swear by everything, and as though by necessity, at the same time, a school of studious detractors, who will suspiciously question everything, or throw out suggestions of disparagement, is at all events, a proof of greatness, the countersign of undoubted genius, and an assurance of lasting fame. R. L. Stevenson has certainly secured this. Time will tell what of virtue there is with either party. For me, who knew Stevenson, and loved him, as finding in the sweet-tempered, brave, and in some things, most generous man, what gave at once tone and elevation to the artist, I would fain indicate here my impressions of him and his genius – impressions that remain almost wholly uninfluenced by the vast mass of matter about him that the press now turns out. Books, not to speak of articles, pour forth about him – about his style, his art, his humour and his characters – aye, and even about his religion.

Miss Simpson follows Mr Bellyse Baildon with the *Edinburgh Days*, Miss Moyes Black comes on with her picture in the *Famous Scots*, and Professor Raleigh succeeds her; Mr Graham Balfour follows with his *Life*; Mr Kelman's volume about his Religion comes next, and that is reinforced by more familiar letters and *Table Talk*, by Lloyd Osbourne and Mrs Strong, his step-children; Mr J. Hammerton then comes on handily with *Stevensoniana* – fruit lovingly gathered from many and far fields, and garnered with not a little tact and taste, and catholicity; Miss Laura Stubbs then presents us with her touching *Stevenson's Shrine: the Record of a Pilgrimage*; and Mr Sidney Colvin is now busily at work on his *Life of Stevenson*, which must do not a little to enlighten and to settle many questions.

Curiosity and interest grow as time passes; and the places connected with Stevenson, hitherto obscure many of them, are now touched with light if not with romance, and are known, by name at all events, to every reader of books. Yes; every place he lived in, or touched at, is worthy of full description if only on account of its associations with him. If there is not a land of Stevenson, as there is a land of Scott, or of Burns, it is due to the fact that he was far-travelled, and in his works painted many scenes: but there are at home—Edinburgh, and Halkerside and Allermuir, Caerketton, Swanston, and Colinton, and Maw Moss and Rullion Green and Tummel, "the *wale* of Scotland," as he named it to me, and the Castletown of Braemar—Braemar in his view coming a good second to Tummel, for starting-points to any curious worshipper who would go the round in Scotland and miss nothing. Mr Geddie's work on *The Home Country of Stevenson* may be found very helpful here.

1. It is impossible to separate Stevenson from his work, because of the imperious personal element in it; and so I shall not now strive to gain the appearance of cleverness by affecting any distinction here. The first thing I would say is, that he was when I knew him—what pretty much to the end he remained—a youth. His outlook on life was boyishly genial and free, despite all his sufferings from ill-health—it was the pride of action, the joy of endurance, the revelry of high spirits, and the sense of victory that most fascinated him; and his theory of life was to take pleasure and give pleasure, without calculation or stint—a kind of boyish grace and bounty never to be overcome or disturbed by outer accident or change. If he was sometimes haunted with the thought of changes through changed conditions or circumstances, as my very old friend, Mr Charles Lowe, has told even of the College days that he was always supposing things to undergo some sea-change into something else, if not "into something rich and strange," this was but to add to his sense of enjoyment, and the power of conferring delight, and the luxuries of variety, as boys do when they let fancy loose. And this always had, with him, an individual reference or return. He was thus constantly, and latterly, half-consciously, trying to interpret himself somehow through all the things which engaged him, and which he so transmogrified—things that especially attracted him and took his fancy. Thus, if it must be confessed, that even in his highest moments, there lingers a touch—if no more than a touch—of self-consciousness which will not allow him to forget manner in matter, it is also true that he is cunningly conveying traits in himself; and the sense of this is often at the root of his sweet, gentle, naove humour. There is, therefore, some truth in the criticisms which assert that even "long John Silver," that fine pirate, with his one leg, was, after all, a shadow of Stevenson himself—the genial buccaneer who did his tremendous murdering with a smile on his face was but

Stevenson thrown into new circumstances, or, as one has said, Stevenson-cum-Henley, so thrown as was also Archer in *Weir of Hermiston*, and more than this, that his most successful women-folk—like Miss Grant and Catriona—are studies of himself, and that in all his heroes, and even heroines, was an unmistakable touch of R. L. Stevenson. Even Mr Baildon rather maladroitly admits that in Miss Grant, the Lord Advocate's daughter, *there is a good deal of the author himself disguised in petticoats*. I have thought of Stevenson in many suits, beside that which included the velvet jacket, but—petticoats!

Youth is autocratic, and can show a grand indifferency: it goes for what it likes, and ignores all else—it fondly magnifies its favourites, and, after all, to a great extent, it is but analysing, dealing with and presenting itself to us, if we only watch well. This is the secret of all prevailing romance: it is the secret of all stories of adventure and chivalry of the simpler and more primitive order; and in one aspect it is true that R. L. Stevenson loved and clung to the primitive and elemental, if it may not be said, as one distinguished writer has said, that he even loved savagery in itself. But hardly could it be seriously held, as Mr I. Zangwill held:

> "That women did not cut any figure in his books springs from this same interest in the elemental. Women are not born, but made. They are a social product of infinite complexity and delicacy. For a like reason Stevenson was no interpreter of the modern. . . . A child to the end, always playing at 'make-believe,' dying young, as those whom the gods love, and, as he would have died had he achieved his centenary, he was the natural exponent in literature of the child."

But there were subtly qualifying elements beyond what Mr Zangwill here recognises and reinforces. That is just about as correct and true as this other deliverance:

> "His Scotch romances have been as over-praised by the zealous Scotsmen who cry 'genius' at the sight of a kilt, and who lose their heads at a waft from the heather, as his other books have been under-praised. The best of all, *The Master of Ballantrae*,

> ends in a bog; and where the author aspires to exceptional subtlety of character-drawing he befogs us or himself altogether. We are so long weighing the brothers Ballantrae in the balance, watching it incline now this way, now that, scrupulously removing a particle of our sympathy from the one brother to the other, to restore it again in the next chapter, that we end with a conception of them as confusing as Mr Gilbert's conception of Hamlet, who was idiotically sane with lucid intervals of lunacy."

If Stevenson was, as Mr Zangwill holds, "the child to the end," and the child only, then if we may not say what Carlyle said of De Quincey: "*Eccovi*, that child has been in hell," we may say, "*Eccovi*, that child has been in unchildlike haunts, and can't forget the memory of them." In a sense every romancer is a child—such was Ludwig Tieck, such was Scott, such was James Hogg, the Ettrick Shepherd. But each is something more—he has been touched with the wand of a fairy, and knows, at least, some of Elfin Land as well as of childhood's home.

The sense of Stevenson's youthfulness seems to have struck every one who had intimacy with him. Mr Baildon writes (p. 21 of his book):

> I would now give much to possess but one of Stevenson's gifts—namely, that extraordinary vividness of recollection by which he could so astonishingly recall, not only the doings, but the very thoughts and emotions of his youth. For, often as we must have communed together, with all the shameless candour of boys, hardly any remark has stuck to me except the opinion already alluded to, which struck me—his elder by some fifteen months—as very amusing, that at sixteen 'we should be men.' *He of all mortals, who was, in a sense, always still a boy!*"

Mr Gosse tells us:

> "He had retained a great deal of the temperament of a child, and it was his philosophy to encourage it. In his dreary passages of bed, when his illness was more than commonly heavy on him, he used to contrive little amusements for himself. He played on the flute, or he modelled little groups and figures in clay."

2. One of the qualifying elements unnoted by Mr Zangwill is simply this, that R. L. Stevenson never lost the strange tint imparted to his youth by the religious influences to which he was subject, and which left their impress and colour on him and all that he did. Henley, in his striking sonnet, hit it when he wrote:

> "A deal of Ariel, just a streak of Puck,
> Much Antony, of Hamlet most of all,
> *And something of the Shorter Catechist.*"

Something! he was a great deal of Shorter Catechist! Scotch Calvinism, its metaphysic, and all the strange whims, perversities, and questionings of "Fate, free-will, foreknowledge absolute," which it inevitably awakens, was much with him—the sense of reprobation and the gloom born of it, as well as the abounding joy in the sense of the elect—the Covenanters and their wild resolutions, the moss-troopers and their dare-devilries—Pentland Risings and fights of Rullion Green; he not only never forgot them, but they mixed themselves as in his very breath of life, and made him a great questioner. How would I have borne myself in this or in that? Supposing I had been there, how would it have been—the same, or different from what it was with those that were there? His work is throughout at bottom a series of problems that almost all trace to this root, directly or indirectly. "There, but for the grace of God, goes John Bradford," said the famous Puritan on seeing a felon led to execution; so with Stevenson. Hence his fondness for tramps, for scamps (he even bestowed special attention and pains on Villon, the poet-scamp); he was rather impatient with poor Thoreau, because he was a purist solitary, and had too little of vice, and, as Stevenson held, narrow in sympathy, and too self-satisfied, and bent only on self-improvement. He held a brief for the honest villain, and leaned to him brotherly. Even the anecdotes he most prizes have a fine look this way—a hunger for completion in achievement, even in the violation of fine humane feeling or morality, and all the time a sense of submission to God's will. "Doctor," said the dying gravedigger in *Old Mortality*, "I hae laid three hunner an' fower score in that kirkyaird, an' had it been His wull," indicating Heaven, "I wad hae likeit weel to hae made oot the fower hunner." That took Stevenson. Listen to what Mr Edmond Gosse tells of his talk, when he found him in a private hotel in Finsbury Circus, London, ready to be put on board a steamer for America, on 21st August, 1887:

> "It was church time, and there was some talk of my witnessing his will, which I could not do because there could be found no other reputable witness, the whole crew of the hotel being at church. 'This,' he said, 'is the way in which our valuable city hotels—packed no doubt with gems and jewellery—are deserted on a Sunday morning. Some bold piratical fellow, defying the spirit of Sabbatarianism, might make a handsome revenue by sacking the derelict hotels between the hours of ten and twelve. One hotel a week would enable such a man to retire in course of a year. A mask might perhaps be worn for the mere fancy of the thing, and to terrify kitchen-maids, but no real disguise would be needful.'"

I would rather agree with Mr Chesterton than with Mr Zangwill here:

> "Stevenson's enormous capacity for joy flowed directly out of his profoundly religious temperament. He conceived himself as an unimportant guest at one eternal and uproarious banquet, and instead of grumbling at the soup, he accepted it with careless gratitude. . . . His gaiety was neither the gaiety of the pagan, nor the gaiety of the *bon vivant*. It was the greater gaiety of the mystic. He could enjoy trifles because there was to him no such thing as a trifle. He was a child who respect-

> ed his dolls because they were the images of the image of God, portraits at only two removes."

Here, then, we have the child crossed by the dreamer and the mystic, bred of Calvinism and speculation on human fate and chance, and on the mystery of temperament and inheritance, and all that flows from these—reprobation, with its dire shadows, assured Election with its joys, etc., etc.

3. If such a combination is in favour of the story-teller up to a certain point, it is not favourable to the highest flights, and it is alien to dramatic presentation pure and simple. This implies detachment from moods and characters, high as well as low, that complete justice in presentation may be done to all alike, and the one balance that obtains in life grasped and repeated with emphasis. But towards his leading characters Stevenson is unconsciously biassed, because they are more or less shadowy projections of himself, or images through which he would reveal one or other side or aspect of his own personality. Attwater is a confessed failure, because it, more than any other, testifies this: he is but a mouth-piece for one side or tendency in Stevenson. If the same thing is not more decisively felt in some other cases, it is because Stevenson there showed the better art o' hidin', and not because he was any more truly detached or dramatic. "Of Hamlet most of all," wrote Henley in his sonnet. The Hamlet in Stevenson—the self-questioning, egotistic, moralising Hamlet—was, and to the end remained, a something alien to bold, dramatic, creative freedom. He is great as an artist, as a man bent on giving to all that he did the best and most distinguished form possible, but not great as a free creator of dramatic power. "Mother," he said as a mere child, "I've drawed a man. Now, will I draw his soul?" He was to the end all too fond to essay a picture of the soul, separate and peculiar. All the Jekyll and Hyde and even Ballantrae conceptions came out of that—and what is more, he always mixed his own soul with the other soul, and could not help doing so.

4. When; therefore, I find Mr Pinero, in lecturing at Edinburgh, deciding in favour of Stevenson as possessed of rare dramatic power, and wondering why he did not more effectively employ it, I can't agree with him; and this because of the presence of a certain

atmosphere in the novels, alien to free play of the individualities presented. Like Hawthorne's, like the works of our great symbolists, they are restricted by a sense of some obtaining conception, some weird metaphysical *weird* or preconception. This is the ground "Ian MacLaren" has for saying that "his kinship is not with Boccaccio and Rabelais, but with Dante and Spenser"—the ground for many remarks by critics to the effect that they still crave from him "less symbol and more individuality"—the ground for the Rev. W. J. Dawson's remark that "he has a powerful and persistent sense of the spiritual forces which move behind the painted shows of life; that he writes not only as a realist but as a prophet, his meanest stage being set with eternity as a background."

Such expressions are fullest justification for what we have here said: it adds, and can only add, to our admiration of Stevenson, as a thinker, seer, or mystic, but the asserting sense of such power can only end in lessening the height to which he could attain as a dramatic artist; and there is much indeed against Mr Pinero's own view that, in the dramas, he finds that "fine speeches" are ruinous to them as acting plays. In the strict sense overfine speeches are yet almost everywhere. David Balfour could never have writ some speeches attributed to him—they are just R. L. Stevenson with a very superficial difference that, when once detected, renders them curious and quaint and interesting, but not dramatic.

CHAPTER XIII—PREACHER AND MYSTIC FABULIST

In reality, Stevenson is always directly or indirectly preaching a sermon—enforcing a moral—as though he could not help it. "He would rise from the dead to preach a sermon." He wrote some first-rate fables, and might indeed have figured to effect as a moralist-fabulist, as truly he was from beginning to end. There was a bit of Bunyan in him as well as of Fsop and Rousseau and Thoreau—the mixture that found coherency in his most peculiarly patient and forbearing temper is what gives at once the quaintness, the freedom, and yet the odd didactic something that is never wanting. I remember a fable about the Devil that might well be brought in to illustrate this here—careful readers who neglect nothing that Stevenson wrote will remember it also and perhaps bear me out here.

But for the sake of the young folks who may yet have some leeway to make up, I shall indulge myself a little by quoting it: and, since I am on that tack, follow it by another which presents Stevenson in his favourite guise of quizzing his own characters, if not for his own advantage certainly for ours, if we would in the least understand the fine moralist-casuistical qualities of his mind and fancy:

> THE DEVIL AND THE INNKEEPER
>
> Once upon a time the devil stayed at an inn, where no one knew him, for they were people whose education had been neglected. He was bent on mischief, and for a time kept everybody by the ears. But at last the innkeeper set a watch upon the devil and took him in the act.
>
> The innkeeper got a rope's end.
>
> "Now I am going to thrash you," said the innkeeper.
>
> "You have no right to be angry with me," said the devil. "I am only the devil, and it is my nature to do wrong."

> "Is that so?" asked the innkeeper.
>
> "Fact, I assure you," said the devil.
>
> "You really cannot help doing ill?" asked the innkeeper.
>
> "Not in the smallest," said the devil, "it would be useless cruelty to thrash a thing like me."
>
> "It would indeed," said the innkeeper.
>
> And he made a noose and hanged the devil.
>
> "There!" said the innkeeper.

The deeper Stevenson goes, the more happily is he inspired. We could scarcely cite anything more Stevensonian, alike in its humour and its philosophy, than the dialogue between Captain Smollett and Long John Silver, entitled *The Persons of the Tale*. After chapter xxxii. of *Treasure Island*, these two puppets "strolled out to have a pipe before business should begin again, and met in an open space not far from the story." After a few preliminaries:

> "You're a damned rogue, my man," said the Captain.
>
> "Come, come, Cap'n, be just," returned the other. "There's no call to be angry with me in earnest. I'm on'y a character in a sea story. I don't really exist."
>
> "Well, I don't really exist either," says the Captain, "which seems to meet that."
>
> "I wouldn't set no limits to what a virtuous character might consider argument," responded Silver. "But I'm the villain of the tale, I am; and speaking as one seafaring man to another, what I want to know is, what's the odds?"
>
> "Were you never taught your catechism?" said the Captain. "Don't you know there's such a thing as an Author?"

> "Such a thing as a Author?" returned John, derisively. "And who better'n me? And the p'int is, if the Author made you, he made Long John, and he made Hands, and Pew, and George Merry—not that George is up to much, for he's little more'n a name; and he made Flint, what there is of him; and he made this here mutiny, you keep such a work about; and he had Tom Redruth shot; and—well, if that's a Author, give me Pew!"
>
> "Don't you believe in a future state?" said Smollett. "Do you think there's nothing but the present sorty-paper?"
>
> "I don't rightly know for that," said Silver, "and I don't see what it's got to do with it, anyway. What I know is this: if there is sich a thing as a Author, I'm his favourite chara'ter. He does me fathoms better'n he does you—fathoms, he does. And he likes doing me. He keeps me on deck mostly all the time, crutch and all; and he leaves you measling in the hold, where nobody can't see you, nor wants to, and you may lay to that! If there is a Author, by thunder, but he's on my side, and you may lay to it!"
>
> "I see he's giving you a long rope," said the Captain. . . .

Stevenson's stories—one and all—are too closely the illustrations by characters of which his essays furnish the texts. You shall not read the one wholly apart from the other without losing something—without losing much of the quaint, often childish, and always insinuating personality of the writer. It is this if fully perceived which would justify one writer, Mr Zangwill, if I don't forget, in saying, as he did say, that Stevenson would hold his place by his essays and not by his novels. Hence there is a unity in all, but a unity found in a root which is ultimately inimical to what is strictly free dramatic creation—creation, broad, natural and unmoral in the highest sense just as nature is, as it is to us, for example, when we speak of Shakespeare, or even Scott, or of Cervantes or Fielding. If

Mr Henley in his irruptive if not spiteful *Pall Mall Magazine* article had made this clear from the high critical ground, then some of his derogatory remarks would not have been quite so personal and offensive as they are.

Stevenson's bohemianism was always restrained and coloured by this. He is a casuistic moralist, if not a Shorter Catechist, as Mr Henley put it in his clever sonnet. He is constantly asking himself about moral laws and how they work themselves out in character, especially as these suggest and involve the casuistries of human nature. He is often a little like Nathaniel Hawthorne, but he hardly follows them far enough and rests on his own preconceptions and predilections, only he does not, like him, get into or remain long in the cobwebby corners—his love of the open air and exercise derived from generations of active lighthouse engineers, out at all times on sea or land, or from Scottish ministers who were fond of composing their sermons and reflecting on the backwardness of human nature as they walked in their gardens or along the hillsides even among mists and storms, did something to save him here, reinforcing natural cheerfulness and the warm desire to give pleasure. His excessive elaboration of style, which grew upon him more and more, giving throughout often a sense of extreme artificiality and of the self-consciousness usually bred of it, is but another incidental proof of this. And let no reader think that I wish here to decry R. L. Stevenson. I only desire faithfully to try to understand him, and to indicate the class or group to which his genius and temperament really belong. He is from first to last the idealistic dreamy or mystical romancer, and not the true idealist or dealer direct with life or character for its own sake. The very beauty and sweetness of his spirit in one way militated against his dramatic success—he really did not believe in villains, and always made them better than they should have been, and that, too, on the very side where wickedness—their natural wickedness—is most available—on the stage. The dreamer of dreams and the Shorter Catechist, strangely united together, were here directly at odds with the creative power, and crossed and misdirected it, and the casuist came in and manoeuvred the limelight—all too like the old devil of the mediaeval drama, who was made only to be laughed at and taken lightly, a buffoon and a laughing-stock indeed. And while he could unveil villainy, as is the case pre-eminently in Huish in the *Ebb-Tide*, he shrank from inflicting the punishments for which untutored human nature looks, and thus he lost one great aid to crude dramatic effect. As to his poems, they are intimately personal in his happiest moments: he deals with separate moods and sentiments, and scarcely ever touches those of a type alien to his own. The defect of his child poems is distinctly that he is everywhere strictly recalling and reproducing his own quaint and wholly exceptional childhood; and children, ordinary, normal, healthy children, will not take to these poems (though grown-ups largely do so), as they would to, say, the *Lilliput Levie* of my old friend, W. B. Rands. Rands showed a great deal of true dramatic play there within his own very narrow limits, as, at all events, adults must conceive them.

Even in his greatest works, in *The Master of Ballantrae* and *Weir of Hermiston*, the special power in Stevenson really lies in subduing his characters at the most critical point for action, to make them prove or sustain his thesis; and in this way the rare effect that he might have secured *dramatically* is largely lost and make-believe substituted, as in the Treasure Search in the end of *The Master of Ballantrae*. The powerful dramatic effect he might have had in his *dinouement* is thus completely sacrificed. The essence of the drama for the stage is that the work is for this and this alone—dialogue and everything being only worked rightly when it bears on, aids, and finally secures this in happy completeness.

In a word, you always, in view of true dramatic effect, see Stevenson himself too clearly behind his characters. The "fine speeches" Mr Pinero referred to trace to the intrusion behind the glass of a part-quicksilvered portion, which cunningly shows, when the glass is moved about, Stevenson himself behind the character, as we have said already. For long he shied dealing with women, as though by a true instinct. Unfortunately for him his image was as clear behind *Catriona*, with the discerning, as anywhere else; and this, alas! too far undid her as an independent, individual character, though traits like those in her author were attractive. The constant effort to relieve the sense of this affords him the most admirable openings for the display of his exquisite style, of which he seldom or never fails to make the very most in this regard; but the necessity laid upon him to aim at securing a sense of relief by this is precisely the same as led him to write the overfine speeches in the plays, as Mr Pinero found and pointed out at Edinburgh: both defeat the true end, but in the written book mere art of style and a naovete and a certain sweetness of temper conceal the lack of nature and creative spontaneity; while on the stage the descriptions, saving reflections and fine asides, are ruthlessly cut away under sheer stage necessities, or, if left, but hinder the action; and art of this kind does not there suffice to conceal the lack of nature.

More clearly to bring out my meaning here and draw aid from comparative illustration, let me take my old friend of many years, Charles Gibbon. Gibbon was poor, very poor, in intellectual subtlety compared with Stevenson; he had none of his sweet, quaint, original fancy; he was no casuist; he was utterly void of power in the subdued humorous twinkle or genial by-play in which Stevenson excelled. But he has more of dramatic power, pure and simple, than Stevenson had—his novels—the best of them—would far more easily yield themselves to the ordinary purposes of the ordinary playwright. Along with conscientiousness, perception, penetration, with the dramatist must go a certain indescribable common-sense commonplaceness—if I may name it so—protection against vagary and that over-refined egotism and self-confession which is inimical to the drama and in which the Stevensonian type all too largely abounds for successful dramatic production. Mr Henley perhaps put it too strongly when he said that what was supremely of interest to R. L. Stevenson was Stevenson himself; but he indicates the tendency, and that tendency is inimical to strong, broad, effective and varied dramatic presentation. Water cannot rise above its own level; nor can minds of this type go freely out of themselves in a grandly healthy, unconscious, and unaffected way, and this is the secret of the dramatic spirit, if it be not, as Shelley said, the secret of morals, which Stevenson, when he passed away, was but on the way to attain. As we shall see, he had risen so far above it, subdued it, triumphed over it, that we really cannot guess what he might have attained had but more years been given him. For the last attainment of the loftiest and truest genius is precisely this—to gain such insight of the real that all else becomes subsidiary. True simplicity and the abiding relief and enduring power of true art with all classes lies here and not elsewhere. Cleverness, refinement, fancy, and invention, even sublety of intellect, are practically nowhere in this sphere without this.

CHAPTER XIV – STEVENSON AS DRAMATIST

In opposition to Mr Pinero, therefore, I assert that Stevenson's defect in spontaneous dramatic presentation is seen clearly in his novels as well as in his plays proper.

In writing to my good friend, Mr Thomas M'Kie, Advocate, Edinburgh, telling him of my work on R. L. Stevenson and the results, I thus gathered up in little the broad reflections on this point, and I may perhaps be excused quoting the following passages, as they reinforce by a new reference or illustration or two what has just been said:

> "Considering his great keenness and force on some sides, I find R. L. Stevenson markedly deficient in grip on other sides – common sides, after all, of human nature. This was so far largely due to a dreamy, mystical, so far perverted and, so to say, often even inverted casuistical, fatalistic morality, which would not allow him scope in what Carlyle would have called a healthy hatred of fools and scoundrels; with both of which classes – vagabonds in strictness – he had rather too much of a sneaking sympathy. Mr Pinero was wrong – totally and incomprehensibly wrong – when he told the good folks of Edinburgh at the Philosophical Institution, and afterwards at the London Birkbeck Institution, that it was lack of concentration and care that made R. L. Stevenson a failure as a dramatist. No: it was here and not elsewhere that the failure lay. R. L. Stevenson was himself an unconscious paradox – and sometimes he realised it – his great weakness from this point of view being that he wished to show strong and original by making the villain the hero of the piece as well. Now, *that*, if it may, by clever manipulation and dexterity, be made to do in a novel, most certainly it will not do on the stage – more especially if it is done consciously and, as it were, of *malice prepense*;

because, for one thing, there is in the theatre a very varied yet united audience which has to give a simultaneous and immediate verdict—an audience not inclined to some kinds of overwrought subtleties and casuistries, however clever the technique. If *The Master of Ballantrae* (which has some highly dramatic scenes and situations, if it is not in itself substantially a drama) were to be put on the stage, the playwright, if wisely determined for success, would really have—not in details, but in essential conception—to kick R. L. Stevenson in his most personal aim out of it, and take and present a more definite moral view of the two villain-heroes (brothers, too); improve and elevate the one a bit if he lowered the other, and not wobble in sympathy and try to make the audience wobble in sympathy also, as R. L. Stevenson certainly does. As for *Beau Austin*, it most emphatically, in view of this, should be re-writ—re-writ especially towards the ending—and the scandalous Beau tarred and feathered, metaphorically speaking, instead of walking off at the end in a sneaking, mincing sort of way, with no more than a little momentary twinge of discomfort at the wreck and ruin he has wrought, for having acted as a selfish, snivelling poltroon and coward, though in fine clothes and with fine ways and fine manners, which only, from our point of view, make matters worse. It is, with variations I admit, much the same all through: R. L. Stevenson felt it and confessed it about the *Ebb-Tide*, and Huish, the cockney hero and villain; but the sense of healthy disgust, even at the vile Huish, is not emphasised in the book as it would have demanded to be for the stage—the audience would not have stood it, and the more mixed and varied, the less would it have stood it—not at all; and his relief of style and fine or finished speeches would not *there* in the least have told. This is demanded of the drama—that at once it satisfies a certain crude

> something subsisting under all outward glosses and veneers that might be in some a lively sense of right and wrong—the uprisal of a conscience, in fact, or in others a vague instinct of proper reward or punishment, which will even cover and sanction certain kinds of revenge or retaliation. The one feeling will emerge most among the cultured, and the other among the ruder and more ignorant; but both meet immediately on beholding action and the limits of action on the demand for some clear leading to what may be called Providential equity—each man undoubtedly rewarded or punished, roughly, according to his deserts, if not outwardly then certainly in the inner torments that so often lead to confessions. There it is—a radical fact of human nature—as radical as any reading of trait or determination of character presented—seen in the Greek drama as well as in Shakespeare and the great Elizabethan dramatists, and in the drama-transpontine and others of to-day. R. L. Stevenson was all too casuistical (though not in the exclusively bad sense) for this; and so he was not dramatic, though *Weir of Hermiston* promised something like an advance to it, and *St Ives* did, in my idea, yet more."

The one essential of a *dramatic* piece is that, by the interaction of character and incident (one or other may be preponderating, according to the type and intention of the writer) all naturally leads up to a crisis in which the moral motives, appealed to or awakened by the presentation of the play, are justified. Where this is wanting the true leading and the definite justification are wanting. Goethe failed in this in his *Faust*, resourceful and far-seeing though he was—he failed because a certain sympathy is awakened for Mephistopheles in being, so to say, chivied out of his bargain, when he had complied with the terms of the contract by Faust; and Gounod in his opera does exactly for "immediate dramatic effect," what we hold it would be necessary to do for R. L. Stevenson. Goethe, with his casuistries which led him to allegory and all manner of overdone symbolisms and perversions in the Second Part, is set aside and a true crisis and close is found by Gounod through simply sending Marguerite above and Faust below, as, indeed, Faust had agreed by solemn compact with Mephistopheles that it should be. And to come to another illustration from our own times, Mr Bernard Shaw's very clever and all too ingenious and over-subtle *Man and Superman* would, in my idea, and for much the same reason, be an utterly ineffective and weak piece on the stage, however carefully handled and however clever the setting—the reason lying in the egotistic upsetting of the "personal equation" and the theory of life that lies behind all—tinting it with strange and even *outri* colours. Much the same has to be said of most of what are problem-plays—several of Ibsen's among the rest.

Those who remember the Fairy opera of *Hansel and Gretel* on the stage in London, will not have forgotten in the witching memory of all the charms of scenery and setting, how the scene where the witch of the wood, who was planning out the baking of the little hero and heroine in her oven, having "fatted" them up well, to make sweet her eating of them, was by the coolness and cleverness of the heroine locked in her own oven and baked there, literally brought down the house. She received exactly what she had planned to give those children, whom their own cruel parents had unwittingly, by losing the children in the wood, put into her hands. Quaint, naove, half-grotesque it was in conception, yet the truth of all drama was there actively exhibited, and all casuistic pleading of excuses of some sort, even of justification for the witch (that it was her nature; heredity in her aworking, etc., etc.) would have not only been out of place, but hotly resented by that audience. Now, Stevenson, if he could have made up his mind to have the witch locked in her own oven, would most assuredly have tried some device to get her out by some fairy witch-device or magic slide at the far end of it, and have proceeded to paint for us the changed character that she was after she had been so outwitted by a child, and her witchdom proved after all of little effect. He would have put probably some of the most effective moralities into her mouth if indeed he would not after all have made the witch a triumph on his early principle of bad-heartedness being strength. If this is the sort of falsification which the play demands, and is of all tastes the most ungrateful, then, it is clear, that for full effect of the drama it is essential to it; but what is primary in it is the direct answering to certain immediate and instinctive demands in common human nature, the doing of which is far more effective than no end of deep philosophy to show how much better human nature would be if it were not just quite thus constituted. "Concentration," says Mr Pinero, "is first, second, and last in it," and he goes on thus, as reported in the *Scotsman*, to show Stevenson's defect and mistake and, as is not, of course, unnatural, to magnify the greatness and grandeur of the style of work in which he has himself been so successful.

> "If Stevenson had ever mastered that art—and I do not question that if he had properly conceived it he had it in him to master it—he might have found the stage a gold mine, but he would have found, too, that it is a gold mine which cannot be worked in a smiling, sportive, half-contemptuous spirit, but only in the sweat of the brain, and with every mental nerve and sinew strained to its uttermost. He would have known that no ingots are to be got out of this mine, save after sleepless nights, days of gloom and discouragement, and other days, again, of feverish toil, the result of which proves in the end to be misapplied and has to be thrown to the winds. . . . When you take up a play-book (if ever you do take one up) it strikes you as being a very trifling thing—a mere insubstantial pamphlet beside the imposing bulk of the latest six-shilling novel. Little do you guess that every page of the play has cost more care, severer mental tension, if not more actual manual labour, than any chapter of a novel, though it be fifty pages long. It is the height of the author's art, according to the old maxim, that the ordinary spectator should never be clearly conscious of the skill and travail that have gone to the making of the finished product. But the artist who would achieve a like feat must realise its difficulties, or what are his chances of success?"

But what I should, in little, be inclined to say, in answer to the "concentration" idea is that, unless you have first some firm hold on the broad bed-rock facts of human nature specially appealed to or called forth by the drama, you may concentrate as much as you please, but you will not write a successful acting drama, not to speak of a great one. Mr Pinero's magnifications of the immense effort demanded from him must in the end come to mean that he himself does not instinctively and with natural ease and spontaneity secure this, but secures it only after great conscious effort; and hence, perhaps, it is that he as well as so many other modern playwrights fall so far behind alike in the amount turned out, and also in its quality as compared with the products of many playwrights in the past.

The problem drama, in every phase and turn of it, endeavours to dispense with these fundamental demands implied in the common and instinctive sense or consciousness of the mass of men and women, and to substitute for that interest something which will artificially supersede it, or, at any rate, take its place. The interest is transferred from the crises necessarily worked up to in the one case, with all of situation and dialogue directed to it, and without which it would not be strictly explicable, to something abnormal, odd, artificial or inverted, or exceptional in the characters themselves. Having thus, instead of natural process and sequence, if we may put it so, the problem dramatist has a double task—he must gain what unity he can, and reach such crises as he may by artificial aids and inventions which the more he uses the more makes natural simplicity unattainable; and next he must reduce and hide as far as he can the abnormality he has, after all, in the long run, created and presented. He cannot maintain it to the full, else his work would become a mere medical or psychological treatise under the poorest of disguises; and the very necessity for the action and reaction of characters upon each other is a further element against him. In a word no one character can stand alone, and cannot escape influencing others, and also the action. Thus it is that he cannot isolate as a doctor does his patient for scientific examination. The healthy and normal must come in to modify on all sides what is presented of unhealthy and abnormal, and by its very presence expose the other, while at the same time it, by its very presence, ministers improvement, exactly as the sunlight disperses mist and all unhealthy vapours, germs, and microbes.

The problem dramatist, in place of broad effect and truth to nature, must find it in stress of invention and resource of that kind. Thus care and concentration must be all in all with him—he must never let himself go, or get so interested and taken with his characters that *they*, in a sense, control or direct him. He is all too conscious a "maker" and must pay for his originality by what in the end is really painful and overweighted work. This, I take it, is the reason why so many of the modern dramatists find their work so hard, and are, comparatively, so slow in the production of it, while they would fain, by many devices, secure the general impression or appeal made to all classes alike by the natural or what we may call spontaneous drama, they are yet, by the necessity of subject matter and methods of dealing with it, limited to the real interest of a special class—to whom is finally given up what was meant for mankind—and the troublesome and trying task laid on them, to try as best they may to reconcile two really conflicting tendencies which cannot even by art be reconciled but really point different ways and tend to different ends. As the impressionist and the pre-Raphaelite, in the sister-art of painting cannot be combined and reconciled in one painter—so it is here; by conception and methods they go different ways, and if they *seek* the same end, it is by opposing processes—the original conception alike of nature and of art dictating the process.

As for Stevenson, it was no lack of care or concentration in anything that he touched; these two were never lacking, but because his subtlety, mystical bias and dreaminess, and theorising on human nature made this to him impossible. He might have concentrated as much as he pleased, concentrated as much as even Mr Pinero desires, but he would not have made a successful drama, because he was Robert Louis Stevenson, and not Mr Pinero, and too long, as he himself confessed, had a tendency to think bad-heartedness was strength; while the only true and enduring joy attainable in this world—whether by deduction from life itself, or from *impressions* of art or of the drama, is simply the steady, unassailable, and triumphant consciousness that it is not so, but the reverse, that goodness and self-sacrifice and self-surrender are the only strength in the universe. Just as Byron had it with patriotism:—

> "Freedom's battle once begun,
> Bequeathed from bleeding sire to son,
> Tho' baffled oft is ever won."

To go consciously either in fiction or in the drama for bad-heartedness as strength, is to court failure—the broad, healthy, human heart, thank Heaven, is so made as to resent the doctrine; and if a fiction or a play based on this idea for the moment succeeds, it can only be because of strength in other elements, or because of partial blindness and partially paralysed moral sense in the case of those who accept it and joy in it. If Mr Pinero directly disputes this, then he and I have no common standing-ground, and I need not follow the matter any further. Of course, the dramatist may, under mistaken sympathy and in the midst of complex and bewildering concatenations, give wrong readings to his audience, but he must not be always doing even that, or doing it on principle or system, else his work, however careful and concentrated, will before long share the fate of the Stevenson-Henley dramas confessedly wrought when the authors all too definitely held bad-heartedness was strength.

CHAPTER XV – THEORY OF GOOD AND EVIL

We have not hitherto concerned ourselves, in any express sense, with the ethical elements involved in the tendency now dwelt on, though they are, of necessity, of a very vital character. We have shown only as yet the effect of this mood of mind on dramatic intention and effort. The position is simply that there is, broadly speaking, the endeavour to eliminate an element which is essential to successful dramatic presentation. That element is the eternal distinction, speaking broadly, between good and evil – between right and wrong – between the secret consciousness of having done right, and the consciousness of mere strength and force in certain other ways.

Nothing else will make up for vagueness and cloudiness here – no technical skill, no apt dialogue nor concentration, any more than "fine speeches," as Mr Pinero calls them. Now the dramatic demand and the ethical demand here meet and take each other's hands, and will not be separated. This is why Mr Stevenson and Mr Henley – young men of great talent, failed – utterly failed – they thought they could make a hero out of a shady and dare-devil yet really cowardly villain generally – and failed.

The spirit of this is of the clever youth type – all too ready to forego the moral for the sake of the fun any day of the week, and the unthinking selfishness and self-enjoyment of youth – whose tender mercies are often cruel, are transcendent in it. As Stevenson himself said, they were young men then and fancied bad-heartedness was strength. Perhaps it was a sense of this that made R. L. Stevenson speak as he did of the *Ebb-Tide* with Huish the cockney in it, after he was powerless to recall it; which made him say, as we have seen, that the closing chapters of *The Master of Ballantrae* "*shame, and perhaps degrade, the beginning*." He himself came to see then the great error; but, alas! it was too late to remedy it – he could but go forward to essay new tales, not backward to put right errors in what was done.

Did Mr William Archer have anything of this in his mind and the far-reaching effects on this side, when he wrote the following:

> "Let me add that the omission with which, in 1885, I mildly reproached him—the omission to tell what he knew to be an essential part of the truth about life—was abundantly made good in his later writings. It is true that even in his final philosophy he still seems to me to underrate, or rather to shirk, the significance of that most compendious parable which he thus relates in a letter to Mr Henry James:—'Do you know the story of the man who found a button in his hash, and called the waiter? "What do you call that?" says he. "Well," said the waiter, "what d'you expect? Expect to find a gold watch and chain?" Heavenly apologue, is it not?' Heavenly, by all means; but I think Stevenson relished the humour of it so much that he 'smiling passed the moral by.' In his enjoyment of the waiter's effrontery, he forgot to sympathise with the man (even though it was himself) who had broken his teeth upon the harmful, unnecessary button. He forgot that all the apologetics in the world are based upon just this audacious paralogism."

Many writers have done the same—and not a few critics have hinted at this: I do not think any writer has got at the radical truth of it more directly, decisively, and clearly than "J. F. M.," in a monthly magazine, about the time of Stevenson's death; and the whole is so good and clear that I must quote it—the writer was not thinking of the drama specially; only of prose fiction, and this but makes the passage the more effective and apt to my point.

> "In the outburst of regret which followed the death of Robert Louis Stevenson, one leading journal dwelt on his too early removal in middle life 'with only half his message delivered.' Such a phrase may have been used in the mere cant of modern journalism. Still it set one questioning what was Stevenson's message, or at least that part of it which we had time given us to hear.

"Wonderful as was the popularity of the dead author, we are inclined to doubt whether the right appreciation of him was half as wide. To a certain section of the public he seemed a successful writer of boys' books, which yet held captive older people. Now, undoubtedly there was an element (not the highest) in his work which fascinated boys. It gratified their yearning for adventure. To too large a number of his readers, we suspect, this remains Stevenson's chief charm; though even of those there were many able to recognise and be thankful for the literary power and grace which could serve up their sanguinary diet so daintily.

"Most of Stevenson's titles, too, like *Treasure Island*, *Kidnapped*, and *The Master of Ballantrae*, tended to foster delusion in this direction. The books were largely bought for gifts by maiden aunts, and bestowed as school prizes, when it might not have been so had their titles given more indication of their real scope and tendency.

"All this, it seems to us, has somewhat obscured Stevenson's true power, which is surely that of an arch-delineator of 'human nature' and of the devious ways of men. As we read him we feel that we have our finger on the pulse of the cruel politics of the world. He has the Shakespearean gift which makes us recognise that his pirates and his statesmen, with their violence and their murders and their perversions of justice, are swayed by the same interests and are pulling the same strings and playing on the same passions which are at work in quieter methods around ourselves. The vast crimes and the reckless bloodshed are nothing more nor less than stage effects used to accentuate for the common eye what the seer can detect without them.

"And reading him from this standpoint, Stevenson's 'message' (so far as it was delivered) appears to be that of utter gloom—the creed that good is always overcome by evil. We do not mean in the sense that good always suffers through evil and is frequently crucified by evil. That is only the sowing of the martyr's blood, which is, we know, the seed of the Church. We should not have marvelled in the least that a genius like Stevenson should rebel against mere external 'happy endings,' which, being in flat contradiction to the ordinary ways of Providence, are little short of thoughtless blasphemy against Providence. But the terrible thing about the Stevenson philosophy of life is that it seems to make evil overcome good in the sense of absorbing it, or perverting it, or at best lowering it. When good and evil come in conflict in one person, Dr Jekyll vanishes into Mr Hyde. The awful Master of Ballantrae drags down his brother, though he seems to fight for his soul at every step. The sequel to *Kidnapped* shows David Balfour ready at last to be hail-fellow-well-met with the supple Prestongrange and the other intriguers, even though they had forcibly made him a partner to their shedding of innocent blood.

"Is it possible that this was what Stevenson's experience of real life had brought him? Fortunate himself in so many respects, he was yet one of those who turn aside from the smooth and sunny paths of life, to enter into brotherly sympathy and fellowship with the disinherited. Is this, then, what he found on those darker levels? Did he discover that triumphant hypocrisy treads down souls as well as lives?

"We cannot doubt that it often does so; and it is well that we should see this sometimes, to make us strong to contend with evil before it works out this, its worst mischief, and to rouse us from the easy optimist laziness which sits idle while others are being wronged, and bids them believe 'that all will come right in the end,' when it is our direct duty to do our utmost to make it 'come right' to-day.

"But to show us nothing but the gloomy side, nothing but the weakness of good, nothing but the strength of evil, does not inspire us to contend for the right, does not inform us of the powers and weapons with which we might so contend. To gaze at unqualified and inevitable moral defeat will but leave us to the still worse laziness of pessimism, uttering its discouraging and blasphemous cry, 'It does not matter; nothing will ever come right!'

"Shakespeare has shown us—and never so nobly as in his last great creation of *The Tempest*—that a man has one stronghold which none but himself can deliver over to the enemy—that citadel of his own conduct and character, from which he can smile supreme upon the foe, who may have conquered all down the line, but must finally make pause there.

"We must remember that *The Tempest* was Shakespeare's last work. The genuine consciousness of the possible triumph of the moral nature against every assault is probably reserved for the later years of life, when, somewhat withdrawn from the passions of its struggle, we become those lookers-on who see most of the game. Strange fate is it that so much of our genius vanishes into the great silence before those later years are reached!"

Stevenson was too late in awakening fully to the tragic error to which short-sighted youth is apt to wander that "bad-heartedness is strength." And so, from this point of view, to our sorrow, he too much verified Goethe's saw that "simplicity (not artifice) and repose are the acme of art, and therefore no youth can be a master." In fact, he might very well from another side, have taken one of Goethe's fine sayings as a motto for himself:

> "Greatest saints were ever most kindly-hearted to sinners;
> Here I'm a saint with the best; sinners I never could hate." [7]

Stevenson's own verdict on *Deacon Brodie* given to a *New York Herald* reporter on the author's arrival in New York in September 1887, on the *Ludgate Hill*, is thus very near the precise truth: "The piece has been all overhauled, and though I have no idea whether it will please an audience, I don't think either Mr Henley or I are ashamed of it. *But we were both young men when we did that, and I think we had an idea that bad-heartedness was strength.*"

If Mr Henley in any way confirmed R. L. Stevenson in this perversion, as I much fear he did, no true admirer of Stevenson has much to thank him for, whatever claims he may have fancied he had to Stevenson's eternal gratitude. He did Stevenson about the very worst turn he could have done, and aided and abetted in robbing us and the world of yet greater works than we have had from his hands. He was but condemning himself when he wrote some of the detractory things he did in the *Pall Mall Magazine* about the *Edinburgh Edition*, etc. Men are mirrors in which they see each other: Henley, after all, painted himself much more effectively in that now notorious *Pall Mall Magazine* article than he did R. L. Stevenson. Such is the penalty men too often pay for wreaking paltry revenges—writing under morbid memories and narrow and petty grievances—they not only fail in truth and impartiality, but inscribe a kind of grotesque parody of themselves in their effort to make their subject ridiculous, as he did, for example, about the name Lewis=Louis, and various other things.

R. L. Stevenson's fate was to be a casuistic and mystic moralist at bottom, and could not help it; while, owing to some kink or twist, due, perhaps, mainly to his earlier sufferings, and the teachings he then received, he could not help giving it always a turn to what he himself called "tail-foremost" or inverted morality; and it was not till near the close that he fully awakened to the fact that here he was false to the truest canons at once of morality and life and art, and that if he pursued this course his doom was, and would be, to make his endings "disgrace, or perhaps, degrade his beginnings," and that no true and effective dramatic unity and effect and climax was to be gained. Pity that he did so much on this perverted view of life and world and art: and well it is that he came to perceive it, even though almost too late:—certainly too late for that full presentment of that awful yet gladdening presence of a God's power and equity in this seeming tangled web of a world, the idea which inspired Robert Browning as well as Wordsworth, when he wrote, and gathered it up into a few lines in *Pippa Passes*:

"The year's at the spring,
And day's at the morn;
Morning's at seven;
The hillsides dew-pearled;

The lark's on the wing;
The snail's on the thorn:
God's in His heaven,
All's right with the world.

. . . .

"All service ranks the same with God,
If now, as formerly he trod
Paradise, His presence fills
Our earth, each only as God wills
Can work—God's puppets best and worst,
Are we; there is no last or first."

It shows what he might have accomplished, had longer life been but allowed him.

CHAPTER XVI – STEVENSON'S GLOOM

The problem of Stevenson's gloom cannot be solved by any commonplace cut-and-dried process. It will remain a problem only unless (1) his original dreamy tendency crossed, if not warped, by the fatalistic Calvinism which was drummed into him by father, mother, and nurse in his tender years, is taken fully into account; then (2) the peculiar action on such a nature of the unsatisfying and, on the whole, distracting effect of the bohemian and hail-fellow-well-met sort of ideal to which he yielded, and which has to be charged with much; and (3) the conflict in him of a keenly social animus with a very strong egotistical effusiveness, fed by fancy, and nourished by the enforced solitariness inevitable in the case of one who, from early years up, suffered from painful, and even crushing, disease.

His text and his sermon – which may be shortly summed in the following sentence – be kind, for in kindness to others lies the only true pleasure to be gained in life; be cheerful, even to the point of egotistic self-satisfaction, for through cheerfulness only is the flow of this incessant kindliness of thought and service possible. He was not in harmony with the actual effect of much of his creative work, though he illustrated this in his life, as few men have done. He regarded it as the highest duty of life to give pleasure to others; his art in his own idea thus became in an unostentatious way consecrated, and while he would not have claimed to be a seer, any more than he would have claimed to be a saint, as he would have held in contempt a mere sybarite, most certainly a vein of unblamable hedonism pervaded his whole philosophy of life. Suffering constantly, he still was always kindly. He encouraged, as Mr Gosse has said, this philosophy by every resource open to him. In practical life, all who knew him declared that he was brightness, naove fancy, and sunshine personified, and yet he could not help always, somehow, infusing into his fiction a pronounced, and sometimes almost fatal, element of gloom. Even in his own case they were not pleasure-giving and failed thus in essence. Some wise critic has said that no man can ever write well creatively of that in which in his early youth he had no knowledge. Always behind Stevenson's latest exercises lies the shadow of this as an unshifting background, which by art may be relieved, but never refined away wholly. He cannot escape from it if he would. Here, too, as George MacDonald has neatly and nicely said: We are the victims of our own past, and often a hand is put forth upon us from behind and draws us into life backward. Here was Stevenson, with his half-hedonistic theories of life, the duty of giving pleasure, of making eyes brighter, and casting sunshine around one wherever one went, yet the creator of gloom for us, when all the world was before him where to choose. This fateful shadow pursued him to the end, often giving us, as it were, the very justificative ground for his own father's despondency and gloom, which the son rather too decisively reproved, while he might have sympathised with it in a stranger, and in that most characteristic letter to his mother, which we have quoted, said that it made his father often seem, to him, to be ungrateful—"*Has the man no gratitude*?" Two selves thus persistently and constantly struggled in Stevenson. He was from this point of view, indeed, his own Dr Jekyll and Mr Hyde, the buoyant, self-enjoying, because pleasure-conferring, man, and at the same time the helpless yet fascinating "dark interpreter" of the gloomy and gloom-inspiring side of life, viewed from the point of view of dominating character and inherited influence. When he reached out his hand with desire of pleasure-conferring, lo and behold, as he wrote, a hand from his forefathers was stretched out, and he was pulled backward; so that, as he has confessed, his endings were apt to shame, perhaps to degrade, the beginnings. Here is something pointing to the hidden and secret springs that feed the deeper will and bend it to their service. Individuality itself is but a mirror, which by its inequalities transforms things to odd shapes. Hawthorne confessed to something of this sort. He, like Stevenson, suffered much in youth, if not from disease then through accident, which kept him long from youthful company. At a time when he should have been running free with other boys, he had to be lonely, reading what books he could lay his hands on, mostly mournful and puritanic, by the borders of lone Sebago Lake. He that hath once in youth been touched by this Marah-rod of bitterness will not easily escape from it, when he essays in later years to paint life and the world as he sees them; nay, the hand, when he deems himself freest, will be laid upon him from behind, if not to pull him, as MacDonald has said, into life backward, then to make him a mournful witness of having once been touched by the Marah-rod, whose bitterness again declares itself and wells out its bitterness when set even in the rising and the stirring of the waters.

Such is our view of the "gloom" of Stevenson—a gloom which well might have justified something of his father's despondency. He struggles in vain to escape from it—it narrows, it fatefully hampers and limits the free field of his art, lays upon it a strange atmosphere, fascinating, but not favourable to true dramatic breadth and force, and spontaneous natural simplicity, invariably lending a certain touch of weakness, inconsistency, and inconclusiveness to his endings; so that he himself could too often speak of them afterwards as apt to "shame, perhaps to degrade, the beginnings." This is what true dramatic art should never do. In the ending all that may raise legitimate question in the process—all that is confusing, perplexing in the separate parts—is met, solved, reconciled, at least in a way satisfactory to the general, or ordinary mind; and thus such unity is by it so gained and sealed, that in no case can the true artist, whatever faults may lie in portions of the process-work, say of his endings that "they shame, perhaps degrade, the beginning." Wherever this is the case there will be "gloom," and there will also be a sad, tormenting sense of something wanting. "The evening brings a 'hame';" so should it be here—should it especially be in a dramatic work. If not, "We start; for soul is wanting there;" or, if not soul, then the last halo of the soul's serene triumph. From this side, too, there is another cause for the undramatic character, in the stricter sense of Stevenson's work generally: it is, after all, distressful, unsatisfying, egotistic, for fancy is led at the beck of some pre-established disharmony which throws back an abiding and irremovable gloom on all that went before; and the free spontaneous grace of natural creation which ensures natural simplicity is, as said already, not quite attained.

It was well pointed out in *Hammerton*, by an unanonymous author there quoted (pp. 22, 23), that while in the story, Hyde, the worse one, wins, in Stevenson himself—in his real life—Jekyll won, and not Mr Hyde. This writer, too, might have added that the Master of Ballantrae also wins as well as Beau Austin and Deacon Brodie. R. L. Stevenson's dramatic art and a good deal of his fiction, then, was untrue to his life, and on one side was a lie—it was not in consonance with his own practice or his belief as expressed in life.

In some other matters the test laid down here is not difficult of application. Stevenson, at the time he wrote *The Foreigner at Home*, had seen a good deal; he had been abroad; he had already had experiences; he had had differences with his father about Calvinism and some other things; and yet just see how he applies the standard of his earlier knowledge and observation to England—and by doing so, cannot help exaggerating the outstanding differences, always with an almost provincial accent of unwavering conviction due to his early associations and knowledge. He cannot help paying an excessive tribute to the Calvinism he had formally rejected, in so far as, according to him, it goes to form character—even national character, at all events, in its production of types; and he never in any really effective way glances at what Mr Matthew Arnold called "Scottish manners, Scottish drink" as elements in any way radically qualifying. It is not, of course, that I, as a Scotsman, well acquainted with rural life in some parts of England, as with rural life in many parts of Scotland in my youth, do not heartily agree with him—the point is that, when he comes to this sort of comparison and contrast, he writes exactly as his father would or might have done, with a full consciousness, after all, of the tribute he was paying to the practical outcome on character of the Calvinism in which he so thoroughly believed. It is, in its way, a very peculiar thing—and had I space, and did I believe it would prove interesting to readers in general, I might write an essay on it, with instances—in which case the Address to the Scottish Clergy would come in for more notice, citation and application than it has yet received. But meanwhile just take this little snippet—very characteristic and very suggestive in its own way—and tell me whether it does not justify and bear out fully what I have now said as illustrating a certain side and a strange uncertain limitation in Stevenson:

> "But it is not alone in scenery and architecture that we count England foreign. The constitution of society, the very pillars of the empire, surprise and even pain us. The dull neglected peasant, sunk in matter, insolent, gross and servile, makes a startling contrast to our own long-legged, long-

> headed, thoughtful, Bible-loving ploughman. A week or two in such a place as Suffolk leaves the Scotsman gasping. It seems impossible that within the boundaries of his own island a class should have been thus forgotten. Even the educated and intelligent who hold our own opinions and speak in our own words, yet seem to hold them with a difference or from another reason, and to speak on all things with less interest and conviction. The first shock of English society is like a cold plunge." [8]

As there was a great deal of the "John Bull element" [9] in the little dreamer De Quincey, so there was a great deal, after all, of the rather conceited Calvinistic Scot in R. L. Stevenson, and it is to be traced as clearly in certain of his fictions as anywhere, though he himself would not perhaps have seen it and acknowledged it, as I am here forced now to see it, and to acknowledge it for him.

CHAPTER XVII – PROOFS OF GROWTH

Once again I quote Goethe:

> "Natural simplicity and repose are the acme of art, and hence it follows no youth can be a master."

It has to be confessed that seldom, if ever, does Stevenson naturally and by sheer enthusiasm for subject and characters attain this natural simplicity, if he often attained the counterfeit presentment—artistic and graceful euphony, and new, subtle, and often unexpected concatenations of phrase. Style is much; but it is not everything. We often love Scott the more that he shows loosenesses and lapses here, for, in spite of them, he gains natural simplicity, while not seldom Stevenson, with all his art and fine sense of verbal music, rather misses it. *The Sedulous Ape* sometimes disenchants as well as charms; for occasionally a word, a touch, a turn, sends us off too directly in search of the model; and this operates against the interest as introducing a new and alien series of associations, where, for full effect, it should not be so. And this distraction will be the more insistent, the more knowledge the reader has and the more he remembers; and since Stevenson's first appeal, both by his spirit and his methods, is to the cultured and well read, rather than to the great mass, his "sedulous apehood" only the more directly wars against him as regards deep, continuous, and lasting impression; where he should be most simple, natural and spontaneous; he also is most artificial and involved. If the story-writer is not so much in earnest, not so possessed by his matter that this is allowed to him, how is it to be hoped that we shall be possessed in the reading of it? More than once in *Catriona* we must own we had this experience, directly warring against full possession by the story, and certain passages about Simon Lovat were especially marked by this; if even the first introduction to Catriona herself was not so. As for Miss Barbara Grant, of whom so much has been made by many admirers, she is decidedly clever, indeed too clever by half, and yet her doom is to be a mere *deus ex machinb*, and never do more than just pay a little tribute to Stevenson's own power of *persiflage*, or, if you like, to pay a penalty, poor lass, for the too perfect doing of hat, and really,

really, I could not help saying this much, though, I do believe that she deserved just a wee bit better fate than that.

But we have proofs of great growth, and nowhere are they greater than at the very close. Stevenson died young: in some phases he was but a youth to the last. To a true critic then, the problem is, having already attained so much—a grand style, grasp of a limited group of characters, with fancy, sincerity, and imagination,—what would Stevenson have attained in another ten years had such been but allotted him? It has over and over again been said that, for long he *shied* presenting women altogether. This is not quite true: *Thrawn Janet* was an earlier effort; and if there the problem is persistent, the woman is real. Here also he was on the right road—the advance road. The sex-question was coming forward as inevitably a part of life, and could not be left out in any broad and true picture. This element was effectively revived in *Weir of Hermiston*, and "Weir" has been well said to be sadder, if it does not go deeper than *Denis Duval* or *Edwin Drood*. We know what Dickens and Thackeray could do there; we can but guess now what Stevenson would have done. "Weir" is but a fragment; but, to a wisely critical and unprejudiced mind, it suffices to show not only what the complete work would have been, but what would have inevitably followed it. It shows the turning-point, and the way that was to be followed at the cross-roads—the way into a bigger, realer, grander world, where realism, freed from the dream, and fancy, and prejudice of youth, would glory in achieving the more enduring romance of manhood, maturity and humanity.

Yes; there was growth—undoubted growth. The questioning and severely moral element mainly due to the Shorter Catechism—the tendency to casuistry, and to problems, and wistful introspection—which had so coloured Stevenson's art up to the date of *The Master of Ballantrae*, and made him a great essayist, was passing in the satisfaction of assured insight into life itself. The art would gradually have been transformed also. The problem, pure and simple, would have been subdued in face of the great facts of life; if not lost, swallowed up in the grandeur, pathos, and awe of the tragedy clearly realised and presented.

CHAPTER XVIII – EARLIER DETERMINATIONS AND RESULTS

Stevenson's earlier determination was so distinctly to the symbolic, the parabolic, allegoric, dreamy and mystical – to treatment of the world as an array of weird or half-fanciful existences, witnessing only to certain dim spiritual facts or abstract moralities, occasionally inverted moralities – "tail foremost moralities" as later he himself named them – that a strong Celtic strain in him had been detected and dwelt on by acute critics long before any attention had been given to his genealogy on both sides of the house. The strong Celtic strain is now amply attested by many researches. Such phantasies as *The House of Eld*, *The Touchstone*, *The Poor Thing*, and *The Song of the Morrow*, published along with some fables at the end of an edition of *Dr Jekyll and Mr Hyde*, by Longman's, I think, in 1896, tell to the initiated as forcibly as anything could tell of the presence of this element, as though moonshine, disguising and transfiguring, was laid over all real things and the secret of the world and life was in its glamour: the shimmering and soft shading rendering all outlines indeterminate, though a great idea is felt to be present in the mind of the author, for which he works. The man who would say there is no feeling for symbol – no phantasy or Celtic glamour in these weird, puzzling, and yet on all sides suggestive tales would thereby be declared inept, inefficient – blind to certain qualities that lie near to grandeur in fanciful literature, or the literature of phantasy, more properly.

This power in weird and playful phantasy is accompanied with the gift of impersonating or embodying mere abstract qualities or tendencies in characters. The little early sketch written in June 1875, titled *Good Content*, well illustrates this:

> "Pleasure goes by piping: Hope unfurls his purple flag; and meek Content follows them on a snow-white ass. Here, the broad sunlight falls on open ways and goodly countries; here, stage by stage, pleasant old towns and hamlets border the road, now with high sign-poles, now with high minster spires; the lanes go burrowing under blos-

somed banks, green meadows, and deep woods encompass them about; from wood to wood flock the glad birds; the vane turns in the variable wind; and as I journey with Hope and Pleasure, and quite a company of jolly personifications, who but the lady I love is by my side, and walks with her slim hand upon my arm?

"Suddenly, at a corner, something beckons; a phantom finger-post, a will o' the wisp, a foolish challenge writ in big letters on a brand. And twisting his red moustaches, braggadocio Virtue takes the perilous way where dim rain falls ever, and sad winds sigh. And after him, on his white ass, follows simpering Content.

"Ever since I walk behind these two in the rain. Virtue is all a-cold; limp are his curling feather and fierce moustache. Sore besmirched, on his jackass, follows Content."

The record, entitled *Sunday Thoughts*, which is dated some five days earlier is naove and most characteristic, touched with the phantastic moralities and suggestions already indicated in every sentence; and rises to the fine climax in this respect at the close.

"A plague o' these Sundays! How the church bells ring up the sleeping past! I cannot go in to sermon: memories ache too hard; and so I hide out under the blue heavens, beside the small kirk whelmed in leaves. Tittering country girls see me as I go past from where they sit in the pews, and through the open door comes the loud psalm and the fervent solitary voice of the preacher. To and fro I wander among the graves, and now look over one side of the platform and see the sunlit meadow where the grown lambs go bleating and the ewes lie in the shadow under their heaped fleeces; and now over the other, where the rhododendrons flower fair among the chestnut boles, and far overhead the chestnut lifts its thick leaves and spiry blossom into the dark-blue air. Oh, the height and depth and thickness of the chestnut foliage! Oh, to have wings like a dove, and dwell in the tree's green heart!

. . . .

"A plague o' these Sundays! How the Church bells ring up the sleeping past! Here has a maddening memory broken into my brain. To the door, to the door, with the naked lunatic thought! Once it is forth we may talk of what we dare not entertain; once the intriguing thought has been put to the door I can watch it out of the loophole where, with its fellows, it raves and threatens in dumb show. Years ago when that thought was young, it was dearer to me than all others, and I would speak with it always when I had an hour alone. These rags that so dismally trick forth its madness were once the splendid livery my favour wrought for it on my bed at night. Can you see the device on the badge? I dare not read it there myself, yet have a guess—'*bad ware nicht*'—is not that the humour of it?

. . . .

"A plague o' these Sundays! How the Church bells ring up the sleeping past! If I were a dove and dwelt in the monstrous chestnuts, where the bees murmur all day about the flowers; if I were a sheep and lay on the field there under my comely fleece; if I were one of the quiet dead in the kirkyard—some homespun farmer dead for a long age, some dull hind who followed the plough and handled the sickle for threescore years and ten in the distant past; if I were anything but what I am out here, under the sultry noon, between the deep chestnuts, among the graves, where the fervent voice of the preacher comes to me, thin and solitary, through the open windows; *if I were what I*

> *was yesterday, and what, before God, I shall be again to-morrow, how should I outface these brazen memories, how live down this unclean resurrection of dead hopes!"*

Close associated with this always is the moralising faculty, which is assertive. Take here the cunning sentences on *Selfishness and Egotism*, very Hawthornian yet quite original:

> "An unconscious, easy, selfish person shocks less, and is more easily loved, than one who is laboriously and egotistically unselfish. There is at least no fuss about the first; but the other parades his sacrifices, and so sells his favours too dear. Selfishness is calm, a force of nature; you might say the trees were selfish. But egotism is a piece of vanity; it must always take you into its confidence; it is uneasy, troublesome, seeking; it can do good, but not handsomely; it is uglier, because less dignified, than selfishness itself."

If Mr Henley had but had this clear in his mind he might well have quoted it in one connection against Stevenson himself in the *Pall Mall Magazine* article. He could hardly have quoted anything more apparently apt to the purpose.

In the sphere of minor morals there is no more important topic. Unselfishness is too often only the most exasperating form of selfishness. Here is another very characteristic bit:

> "You will always do wrong: you must try to get used to that, my son. It is a small matter to make a work about, when all the world is in the same case. I meant when I was a young man to write a great poem; and now I am cobbling little prose articles and in excellent good spirits. I thank you. . . . Our business in life is not to succeed, but to continue to fail, in good spirits."

Again:

> "It is the mark of good action that it appears inevitable in the retrospect. We should have been cut-throats to do otherwise. And there's an end.

> We ought to know distinctly that we are damned for what we do wrong; but when we have done right, we have only been gentlemen, after all. There is nothing to make a work about."

The moral to *The House of Eld* is incisive writ out of true experience—phantasy there becomes solemn, if not, for the nonce, tragic:—

> "Old is the tree and the fruit good,
> Very old and thick the wood.
> Woodman, is your courage stout?
> Beware! the root is wrapped about
> Your mother's heart, your father's bones;
> And, like the mandrake, comes with groans."

The phantastic moralist is supreme, jauntily serious, facetiously earnest, most gravely funny in the whole series of *Moral Emblems*.

> "Reader, your soul upraise to see,
> In yon fair cut designed by me,
> The pauper by the highwayside
> Vainly soliciting from pride.
> Mark how the Beau with easy air
> Contemns the anxious rustic's prayer
> And casting a disdainful eye
> Goes gaily gallivanting by.
> He from the poor averts his head . . .
> He will regret it when he's dead."

Now, the man who would trace out step by step and point by point, clearly and faithfully, the process by which Stevenson worked himself so far free of this his besetting tendency to moralised symbolism or allegory into the freer air of life and real character, would do more to throw light on Stevenson's genius, and the obstacles he had had to contend with in becoming a novelist eager to interpret definite times and character, than has yet been done or even faithfully attempted. This would show at once Stevenson's wonderful growth and the saving grace and elasticity of his temperament and genius. Few men who have by force of native genius gone into allegory or moralised phantasy ever depart out of that fateful and enchanted region. They are as it were at once lost and imprisoned in it and kept there as by a spell—the more they struggle for freedom the more surely is the bewitching charm laid upon them—they are but like the fly in amber. It was so with Ludwig Tieck; it was so with Nathaniel Hawthorne; it was so with our own George MacDonald, whose professedly real pictures of life are all informed of this phantasy, which spoils them for what they profess to be, and yet to the discerning cannot disguise what they really are—the attempts of a mystic poet and phantasy writer and allegoristic moralist to walk in the ways of Anthony Trollope or of Mrs Oliphant, and, like a stranger in a new land always looking back (at least by a side-glance, an averted or half-averted face which keeps him from seeing steadily and seeing whole the real world with which now he is fain to deal), to the country from which he came.

Stevenson did largely free himself, that is his great achievement—had he lived, we verily believe, so marked was his progress, he would have been a great and true realist, a profound interpreter of human life and its tragic laws and wondrous compensations—he would have shown how to make the full retreat from fairyland without penalty of too early an escape from it, as was the case with Thomas the Rymer of Ercildoune, and with one other told of by him, and proved that to have been a dreamer need not absolutely close the door to insight into the real world and to art. This side of the subject, never even glanced at by Mr Henley or Mr Zangwill or their *confrhres*, yet demands, and will well reward the closest and most careful attention and thought that can be given to it.

The parabolic element, with the whimsical humour and turn for paradoxical inversion, comes out fully in such a work as *Dr Jekyll and Mr Hyde*. There his humour gives body to his fancy, and reality to the half-whimsical forms in which he embodies the results of deep and earnest speculations on human nature and motive. But even when he is professedly concerned with incident and adventure merely, he manages to communicate to his pages some touch of universality, as of unconscious parable or allegory, so that the reader feels now and then as though some thought, or motive, or aspiration, or weakness of his own were being there cunningly unveiled or presented; and not seldom you feel he has also unveiled and presented some of yours, secret and unacknowledged too.

Hence the interest which young and old alike have felt in *Treasure Island*, *Kidnapped*, and *The Wrecker*—a something which suffices decisively to mark off these books from the mass with which superficially they might be classed.

CHAPTER XIX – EDMUND CLARENCE STEDMAN'S ESTIMATE

It should be clearly remembered that Stevenson died at a little over forty – the age at which severity and simplicity and breadth in art but begin to be attained. If Scott had died at the age when Stevenson was taken from us, the world would have lacked the *Waverley Novels*; if a like fate had overtaken Dickens, we should not have had *A Tale of Two Cities*; and under a similar stroke, Goldsmith could not have written *Retaliation*, or tasted the bitter-sweet first night of *She Stoops to Conquer*. At the age of forty-four Mr Thomas Hardy had probably not dreamt of *Tess of the D'Urbervilles*. But what a man has already done at forty years is likely, I am afraid, to be a gauge as well as a promise of what he will do in the future; and from Stevenson we were entitled to expect perfect form and continued variety of subject, rather than a measurable dynamic gain.

This is the point of view which my friend and correspondent of years ago, Mr Edmund Clarence Stedman, of New York, set out by emphasising in his address, as President of the meeting under the auspices of the Uncut Leaves Society in New York, in the beginning of 1895, on the death of Stevenson, and to honour the memory of the great romancer, as reported in the *New York Tribune*:

> "We are brought together by tidings, almost from the Antipodes, of the death of a beloved writer in his early prime. The work of a romancer and poet, of a man of insight and feeling, which may be said to have begun but fifteen years ago, has ended, through fortune's sternest cynicism, just as it seemed entering upon even more splendid achievement. A star surely rising, as we thought, has suddenly gone out. A radiant invention shines no more; the voice is hushed of a creative mind, expressing its fine imagining in this, our peerless English tongue. His expression was so original and fresh from Nature's treasure-house, so prodigal and various, its too brief flow so consummate through an inborn gift made perfect by

unsparing toil, that mastery of the art by which Robert Louis Stevenson conveyed those imaginings to us so picturesque, yet wisely ordered, his own romantic life—and now, at last, so pathetic a loss which renews

"'The Virgilian cry,
The sense of tears in mortal things,'

that this assemblage has gathered at the first summons, in tribute to a beautiful genius, and to avow that with the putting out of that bright intelligence the reading world experiences a more than wonted grief.

"Judged by the sum of his interrupted work, Stevenson had his limitations. But the work was adjusted to the scale of a possibly long career. As it was, the good fairies brought all gifts, save that of health, to his cradle, and the gift-spoiler wrapped them in a shroud. Thinking of what his art seemed leading to—for things that would be the crowning efforts of other men seemed prentice-work in his case—it was not safe to bound his limitations. And now it is as if Sir Walter, for example, had died at forty-four, with the *Waverley Novels* just begun! In originality, in the conception of action and situation, which, however phantastic, are seemingly within reason, once we breathe the air of his Fancyland; in the union of bracing and heroic character and adventure; in all that belongs to tale-writing pure and simple, his gift was exhaustless. No other such charmer, in this wise, has appeared in his generation. We thought the stories, the fairy tales, had all been told, but 'Once upon a time' meant for him our own time, and the grave and gay magic of Prince Florizel in dingy London or sunny France. All this is but one of his provinces, however distinctive. Besides, how he buttressed his romance with apparent truth! Since Defoe, none had a better right to say: 'There was one thing I determined to do when I began this long story, and that was to tell out everything as it befell.'

"I remember delighting in two fascinating stories of Paris in the time of Frangois Villon, anonymously reprinted by a New York paper from a London magazine. They had all the quality, all the distinction, of which I speak. Shortly afterward I met Mr Stevenson, then in his twenty-ninth year, at a London club, where we chanced to be the only loungers in an upper room. To my surprise he opened a conversation—you know there could be nothing more unexpected than that in London—and thereby I guessed that he was as much, if not as far, away from home as I was. He asked many questions concerning 'the States'; in fact, this was but a few months before he took his steerage passage for our shores. I was drawn to the young Scotsman at once. He seemed more like a New-Englander of Holmes's Brahmin caste, who might have come from Harvard or Yale. But as he grew animated I thought, as others have thought, and as one would suspect from his name, that he must have Scandinavian blood in his veins—that he was of the heroic, restless, strong and tender Viking strain, and certainly from that day his works and wanderings have not belied the surmise. He told me that he was the author of that charming book of gipsying in the Cevennes which just then had gained for him some attentions from the literary set. But if I had known that he had written those two stories of sixteenth-century Paris—as I learned afterwards when they reappeared in the *New Arabian Nights*—I would not have bidden him goodbye as to an 'unfledged comrade,' but would have wished indeed to 'grapple him to my soul with hooks of steel.'

"Another point is made clear as crystal by his life itself. He had the instinct, and he had the courage, to make it the servant, and not the master, of the faculty within him. I say he had the courage, but so potent was his birth-spell that doubtless he could not otherwise. Nothing commonplace sufficed him. A regulation stay-at-home life would have been fatal to his art. The ancient mandate, 'Follow thy Genius,' was well obeyed. Unshackled freedom of person and habit was a prerequisite; as an imaginary artist he felt—nature keeps her poets and story-tellers children to the last—he felt, if he ever reasoned it out, that he must gang his own gait, whether it seemed promising, or the reverse, to kith, kin, or alien. So his wanderings were not only in the most natural but in the wisest consonance with his creative dreams. Wherever he went, he found something essential for his use, breathed upon it, and returned it fourfold in beauty and worth. The longing of the Norseman for the tropic, of the pine for the palm, took him to the South Seas. There, too, strange secrets were at once revealed to him, and every island became an 'Isle of Voices.' Yes, an additional proof of Stevenson's artistic mission lay in his careless, careful, liberty of life; in that he was an artist no less than in his work. He trusted to the impulse which possessed him—that which so many of us have conscientiously disobeyed and too late have found ourselves in reputable bondage to circumstances.

"But those whom you are waiting to hear will speak more fully of all this—some of them with the interest of their personal remembrance—with the strength of their affection for the man beloved by young and old. In the strange and sudden intimacy with an author's record which death makes sure, we realise how notable the list of Stevenson's works produced since 1878; more than a score of books—not fiction alone, but also essays, criticism, biography, drama, even history, and, as I need not remind you, that spontaneous poetry which comes only from a true poet. None can have failed to observe that, having recreated the story of adventure, he seemed in his later fiction to interfuse a subtler purpose—the search for character, the analysis of mind and soul. Just here his summons came. Between the sunrise of one day and the sunset of the next he exchanged the forest study for the mountain grave. There, as he had sung his own wish, he lies 'under the wide and starry sky.' If there was something of his own romance, so exquisitely capricious, in the life of Robert Louis Stevenson, so, also, the poetic conditions are satisfied in his death, and in the choice of his burial-place upon the top of Pala. As for the splendour of that maturity upon which we counted, now never to be fulfilled on sea or land, I say—as once before, when the great New-England romancer passed in the stillness of the night:

"'What though his work unfinished lies? Half bent
The rainbow's arch fades out in upper air,
The shining cataract half-way down the height
Breaks into mist; the haunting strain, that fell
On listeners unaware,
Ends incomplete, but through the starry night
The ear still waits for what it did not tell.'"

Dr Edward Eggleston finely sounded the personal note, and told of having met Stevenson at a hotel in New York. Stevenson was ill when the landlord came to Dr Eggleston and asked him if he should like to meet him. Continuing, he said:

"He was flat on his back when I entered, but I think I never saw anybody grow well in so short a time. It was a soul rather than a body that lay there, ablaze with spiritual fire, good will shining through everywhere. He did not pay me any compliment about my work, and I didn't pay him any about his. We did not burn any of the incense before each other which authors so often think it necessary to do, but we were friends instantly. I am not given to speedy intimacies, but I could not help my heart going out to him. It was a wonderfully invested soul, no hedges or fences across his fields, no concealment. He was a romanticist; I was—well, I don't know exactly what. But he let me into the springs of his romanticism then and there.

"'You go in your boat every day?' he asked. 'You sail? Oh! to write a novel a man must take his life in his hands. He must not live in the town.' And so he spoke, in his broad way, of course, according to the enthusiasm of the moment.

"I can't sound any note of pathos here to-night. Some lives are so brave and sweet and joyous and well-rounded, with such a completeness about them that death does not leave imperfection. He never had the air of sitting up with his own reputation. He let his books toss in the waves of criticism and make their ports if they deserve to. He had no claptrap, no great cause, none of the disease of pruriency which came into fashion with Flaubert and Guy de Maupassant. He simply told his story, with no condescension, taking the readers into his heart and his confidence."

CHAPTER XX – EGOTISTIC ELEMENT AND ITS EFFECTS

From these sources now traced out by us—his youthfulness of spirit, his mystical bias, and tendency to dream—symbolisms leading to disregard of common feelings—flows too often the indeterminateness of Stevenson's work, at the very points where for direct interest there should be decision. In *The Master of Ballantrae* this leads him to try to bring the balances even as regards our interest in the two brothers, in so far justifying from one point of view what Mr Zangwill said in the quotation we have given, or, as Sir Leslie Stephen had it in his second series of the *Studies of a Biographer*:

> "The younger brother in *The Master of Ballantrae*, who is black-mailed by the utterly reprobate master, ought surely to be interesting instead of being simply sullen and dogged. In the later adventures, we are invited to forgive him on the ground that his brain has been affected: but the impression upon me is that he is sacrificed throughout to the interests of the story [or more strictly for the working out of the problem as originally conceived by the author]. The curious exclusion of women is natural in the purely boyish stories, since to a boy woman is simply an incumbrance upon reasonable modes of life. When in *Catriona* Stevenson introduces a love story, it is still unsatisfactory, because David Balfour is so much the undeveloped animal that his passion is clumsy, and his charm for the girl unintelligible. I cannot feel, to say the truth, that in any of these stories I am really among living human beings with whom, apart from their adventures, I can feel any very lively affection or antipathy."

In the *Ebb-Tide* it is, in this respect, yet worse: the three heroes choke each other off all too literally.

In his excess of impartiality he tones down the points and lines that would give the attraction of true individuality to his characters, and instead, would fain have us contented with his liberal, and even over-sympathetic views of them and allowances for them. But instead of thus furthering his object, he sacrifices the whole—and his story becomes, instead of a broad and faithful human record, really a curiosity of autobiographic perversion, and of overweening, if not extravagant egotism of the more refined, but yet over-obtrusive kind.

Mr Baildon thus hits the subjective tendency, out of which mainly this defect—a serious defect in view of interest—arises.

> "That we can none of us be sure to what crime we might not descend, if only our temptation were sufficiently acute, lies at the root of his fondness and toleration for wrong-doers (p. 74).

Thus he practically declines to do for us what we are unwilling or unable to do for ourselves. Interest in two characters in fiction can never, in this artificial way, and if they are real characters truly conceived, be made equal, nor can one element of claim be balanced against another, even at the beck of the greatest artist. The common sentiment, as we have seen, resents it even as it resents lack of guidance elsewhere. After all, the novelist is bound to give guidance: he is an authority in his own world, where he is an autocrat indeed; and can work out issues as he pleases, even as the Pope is an authority in the Roman Catholic world: he abdicates his functions when he declines to lead: we depend on him from the human point of view to guide us right, according to the heart, if not according to any conventional notion or opinion. Stevenson's pause in individual presentation in the desire now to raise our sympathy for the one, and then for the other in *The Master of Ballantrae*, admits us too far into Stevenson's secret or trick of affected self-withdrawal in order to work his problem and to signify his theories, to the loss and utter confusion of his aims from the point of common dramatic and human interest. It is the same in *Catriona* in much of the treatment of James Mohr or More; it is still more so in not a little of the treatment of *Weir of Hermiston* and his son, though there, happily for him and for us, there were the direct restrictions of known fact and history, and clearly an attempt at a truer and broader human conception unburdened by theory or egotistic conception.

Everywhere the problem due to the desire to be overjust, so to say, emerges; and exactly in the measure it does so the source of true dramatic directness and variety is lost. It is just as though Shakespeare were to invent a chorus to cry out at intervals about Iago—"a villain, bad lot, you see, still there's a great deal to be said for him—victim of inheritance, this, that and the other; and considering everything how could you really expect anything else now." Thackeray was often weak from this same tendency—he meant Becky Sharp to be largely excused by the reader on these grounds, as he tries to excuse several others of his characters; but his endeavours in this way to gloss over "wickedness" in a way, do not succeed—the reader does not carry clear in mind as he goes along, the suggestions Thackeray has ineffectually set out and the "healthy hatred of scoundrels" Carlyle talked about has its full play in spite of Thackeray's suggested excuses and palliations, and all in his own favour, too, as a story-wright.

Stevenson's constant habit of putting himself in the place of another, and asking himself how would I have borne myself here or there, thus limited his field of dramatic interest, where the subject should have been made pre-eminently in aid of this effect. Even in Long John Silver we see it, as in various others of his characters, though there, owing to the demand for adventure, and action contributory to it, the defect is not so emphasised. The sense as of a projection of certain features of the writer into all and sundry of his important characters, thus imparts, if not an air of egotism, then most certainly a somewhat constrained, if not somewhat artificial, autobiographical air—in the very midst of action, questions of ethical or casuistical character arise, all contributing to submerging individual character and its dramatic interests under a wave of but half-disguised autobiography. Let Stevenson do his very best—let him adopt all the artificial disguises he may, as writing narrative in the first person, etc., as in *Kidnapped* and *Catriona*, nevertheless, the attentive reader's mind is constantly called off to the man who is actually writing the story. It is as though, after all, all the artistic or artificial disguises were a mere mask, as more than once Thackeray represented himself, the mask partially moved aside, just enough to show a chubby, childish kind of transformed Thackeray face below. This belongs, after all, to the order of self-revelation though under many disguises: it is creation only in its manner of work, not in its essential being—the spirit does not so to us go clean forth of itself, it stops at home, and, as if from a remote and shadowy cave or recess, projects its own colour on all on which it looks.

This is essentially the character of the *mystic*; and hence the justification for this word as applied expressly to Stevenson by Mr Chesterton and others.

> "The inner life like rings of light
> Goes forth of us, transfiguring all we see."

The effect of these early days, with the peculiar tint due to the questionings raised by religious stress and strain, persists with Stevenson; he grows, but he never escapes from that peculiar something which tells of childish influences—of boyish perversions and troubled self-examinations due to Shorter Catechism—any one who would view Stevenson without thought of this, would view him only from the outside—see him merely in dress and outer oddities. Here I see definite and clear heredity. Much as he differed from his worthy father in many things, he was like him in this—the old man like the son, bore on him the marks of early excesses of wistful self-questionings and painful wrestlings with religious problems, that perpetuated themselves in a quaint kind of self-revelation often masked by an assumed self-withdrawal or indifference which to the keen eye only the more revealed the real case. Stevenson never, any more than his father, ceased to be interested in the religious questions for which Scotland has always had a *penchant*—and so much is this the case that I could wish Professor Sidney Colvin would even yet attempt to show the bearing of certain things in that *Address to the Scottish Clergy* written when Stevenson was yet but a young man, on all that he afterwards said and did. It starts in the *Edinburgh Edition* without any note, comment, or explanation whatever, but in that respect the *Edinburgh Edition* is not quite so complete as it might have been made. In view of the point now before us, it is far more important than many of the other trifles there given, and wants explanation and its relation to much in the novels brought out and illustrated. Were this adequately done, only new ground would be got for holding that Stevenson, instead of, as has been said, "seeing only the visible world," was, in truth, a mystical moralist, once and always, whose thoughts ran all too easily into parable and fable, and who, indeed, never escaped wholly from that atmosphere, even when writing of things and characters that seemed of themselves to be wholly outside that sphere. This was the tendency, indeed, that militated against the complete detachment in his case from moral problems and mystical thought, so as to enable him to paint, as it were, with a free hand exactly as he saw; and most certainly not that he saw only the visible world. The mystical element is not directly favourable to creative art. You see in Tolstoy how it arrests and perplexes—how it lays a disturbing check on real presentation—hindering the action, and is not favourable to the loving and faithful representation, which, as Goethe said, all true and high art should be. To some extent you see exactly the same thing in Nathaniel Hawthorne as in Tolstoy. Hawthorne's preoccupations in this way militated against his character-power; his healthy characters who would never have been influenced as he describes by morbid ones yet are not only influenced according to him, but suffer sadly. Phoebe Pyncheon in *The House of the Seven Gables*, gives sunshine to poor Hepzibah Clifford, but is herself never merry again, though joyousness was her natural element. So, doubtless, it would have been with Pansie in *Doctor Dolliver*, as indeed it was with Zenobia and with the hero in the *Marble Faun*. "We all go wrong," said Hawthorne, "by a too strenuous resolution to go right." Lady Byron was to him an intolerably irreproachable person, just as Stevenson felt a little of the same towards Thoreau; notwithstanding that he was the "sunnily-ascetic," the asceticism and its corollary, as he puts it: the passion for individual self-improvement was alien in a way to Stevenson. This is the position of the casuistic mystic moralist and not of the man who sees only the visible world.

Mr Baildon says:

> "Stevenson has many of the things that are wanting or defective in Scott. He has his philosophy of life; he is beyond remedy a moralist, even when his morality is of the kind which he happily calls 'tail foremost,' or as we may say, inverted

> morality. Stevenson is, in fact, much more of a thinker than Scott, and he is also much more of the conscious artist, questionable advantage as that sometimes is. He has also a much cleverer, acuter mind than Scott, also a questionable advantage, as genius has no greater enemy than cleverness, and there is really no greater descent than to fall from the style of genius to that of cleverness. But Stevenson was too critical and alive to misuse his cleverness, and it is generally employed with great effect as in the diabolical ingenuities of a John Silver, or a Master of Ballantrae. In one sense Stevenson does not even belong to the school of Scott, but rather to that of Poe, Hawthorne, and the Brontks, in that he aims more at concentration and intensity, than at the easy, quiet breadth of Scott."

If, indeed, it should not here have been added that Stevenson's theory of life and conduct was not seldom too insistent for free creativeness, for dramatic freedom, breadth and reality.

Now here I humbly think Mr Baldion errs about the cleverness when he criticises Stevenson for the *faux pas* artistically of resorting to the piratic filibustering and the treasure-seeking at the close of *The Master of Ballantrae,* he only tells and tells plainly how cleverness took the place of genius there; as indeed it did in not a few cases—certainly in some points in the Dutch escapade in *Catriona* and in not a few in *Dr Jekyll and Mr Hyde*. The fault of that last story is simply that we seem to hear Stevenson chuckling to himself, "Ah, now, won't they all say at last how clever I am." That too mars the *Merry Men,* whoever wrote them or part wrote them, and *Prince Otto* would have been irretrievably spoiled by this self-conscious sense of cleverness had it not been for style and artifice. In this incessant "see how clever I am," we have another proof of the abounding youthfulness of R. L. Stevenson. If, as Mr Baildon says (p. 30), he had true child's horror of being put in fine clothes in which one must sit still and be good, *Prince Otto* remains attractive in spite of some things and because of his fine clothes. Neither Poe nor Hawthorne could have fallen to the piracy, and treasure-hunting of *The Master of Ballantrae*.

"Far behind Scott in the power of instinctive, irreflective, spontaneous creation of character, Stevenson tells his story with more art and with a firmer grip on his reader." And that is exactly what I, wishing to do all I dutifully can for Stevenson, cannot see. His genius is in nearly all cases pulled up or spoiled by his all too conscious cleverness, and at last we say, "Oh Heavens! if he could and would but let himself go or forget himself what he might achieve." But he doesn't—never does, and therefore remains but a second-rate creator though more and more the stylist and the artist. This is more especially the case at the very points where writers like Scott would have risen and roused all the readers' interest. When Stevenson reaches such points, he is always as though saying "See now how cleverly I'll clear that old and stereotyped style of thing and do something *new*." But there are things in life and human nature, which though they are old are yet ever new, and the true greatness of a writer can never come from evading or looking askance at them or trying to make them out something else than what they really are. No artistic aim or ambition can suffice to stand instead of them or to refine them away. That way lies only cold artifice and frigid lacework, and sometimes Stevenson did go a little too much on this line.

CHAPTER XXI – UNITY IN STEVENSON'S STORIES

The unity in Stevenson's stories is generally a unity of subjective impression and reminiscence due, in the first place, to his quick, almost abnormal boyish reverence for mere animal courage, audacity, and doggedness, and, in the second place, to his theory of life, his philosophy, his moral view. He produces an artificial atmosphere. Everything then has to be worked up to this—kept really in accordance with it, and he shows great art in the doing of this. Hence, though, a quaint sense of sameness, of artificial atmosphere—at once really a lack of spontaneity and of freedom. He is freest when he pretends to nothing but adventure—when he aims professedly at nothing save to let his characters develop themselves by action. In this respect the most successful of his stories is yet *Treasure Island*, and the least successful perhaps *Catriona*, when just as the ambitious aim compels him to pause in incident, the first-person form creates a cold stiffness and artificiality alien to the full impression he would produce upon the reader. The two stories he left unfinished promised far greater things in this respect than he ever accomplished. For it is an indisputable fact, and indeed very remarkable, that the ordinary types of men and women have little or no attraction for Stevenson, nor their commonplace passions either. Yet precisely what his art wanted was due infusion of this very interest. Nothing else will supply the place. The ordinary passion of love to the end he *shies*, and must invent no end of expedients to supply the want. The devotion of the ordinary type, as Thomas Hardy has over and over exhibited it, is precisely what Stevenson wants, to impart to his novels the full sense of reality. The secret of morals, says Shelley, is a going out of self. Stevenson was only on the way to secure this grand and all-sufficing motive. His characters, in a way, are all already like himself, romantic, but the highest is when the ordinary and commonplace is so apprehended that it becomes romantic, and may even, through the artist's deeper perception and unconscious grasp and vision, take the hand of tragedy, and lose nothing. The very atmosphere Stevenson so loved to create was in itself alien to this; and, so far as he went, his most successful revelations were but records of his own limitations.

It is something that he was to the end so much the youth, with fine impulses, if sometimes with sympathies misdirected, and that, too, in such a way as to render his work cold and artificial, else he might have turned out more of the Swift than of the Sterne or Fielding. Prince Otto and Seraphina are from this cause mainly complete failures, alike from the point of view of nature and of art, and the Countess von Rosen is not a complete failure, and would perhaps have been a bit of a success, if only she had made Prince Otto come nearer to losing his virtue. The most perfect in style, perhaps, of all Stevenson's efforts it is yet most out of nature and truth,—a farce, felt to be disguised only when read in a certain mood; and this all the more for its perfections, just as Stevenson would have said it of a human being too icily perfect whom he had met.

On this subject, Mr Baildon has some words so decisive, true, and final, that I cannot refrain from here quoting them:

> "From sheer incapacity to retain it, Prince Otto loses the regard, affection, and esteem of his wife. He goes eavesdropping among the peasantry, and has to sit silent while his wife's honour is coarsely impugned. After that I hold it is impossible for Stevenson to rehabilitate his hero, and, with all his brilliant effects, he fails. . . . I cannot help feeling a regret that such fine work is thrown away on what I must honestly hold to be an unworthy subject. The music of the spheres is rather too sublime an accompaniment for this genteel comedy Princess. A touch of Offenbach would seem more appropriate. Then even in comedy the hero must not be the butt." And it must reluctantly be confessed that in Prince Otto you see in excess that to which there is a tendency in almost all the rest—it is to make up for lack of hold on human nature itself, by resources of style and mere external technical art.

CHAPTER XXII – PERSONAL CHEERFULNESS AND INVENTED GLOOM

Now, it is in its own way surely a very remarkable thing that Stevenson, who, like a youth, was all for *Heiterkeit*, cheerfulness, taking and giving of pleasure, for relief, change, variety, new impressions, new sensations, should, at the time he did, have conceived and written a story like *The Master of Ballantrae*–all in a grave, grey, sombre tone, not aiming even generally at what at least indirectly all art is conceived to aim at–the giving of pleasure: he himself decisively said that it "lacked all pleasurableness, and hence was imperfect in essence." A very strange utterance in face of the oft-repeated doctrine of the essays that the one aim of art, as of true life, is to communicate pleasure, to cheer and to elevate and improve, and in face of two of his doctrines that life itself is a monitor to cheerfulness and mirth. This is true: and it is only explainable on the ground that it is youth alone which can exult in its power of accumulating shadows and dwelling on the dark side–it is youth that revels in the possible as a set-off to its brightness and irresponsibility: it is youth that can delight in its own excess of shade, and can even dispense with sunshine–hugging to its heart the memory of its own often self-created distresses and conjuring up and, with self-satisfaction, brooding over the pain and imagined horrors of a lifetime. Maturity and age kindly bring their own relief–rendering this kind of ministry to itself no longer desirable, even were it possible. *The Master of Ballantrae* indeed marks the crisis. It shows, and effectively shows, the other side of the adventure passion–the desire of escape from its own sombre introspections, which yet, in all its "go" and glow and glitter, tells by its very excess of their tendency to pass into this other and apparently opposite. But here, too, there is nothing single or separate. The device of piracy, etc., at close of *Ballantrae*, is one of the poorest expedients for relief in all fiction.

Will in *Will o' the Mill* presents another. When at the last moment he decides that it is not worth while to get married, the author's then rather incontinent philosophy–which, by-the-bye, he did not himself act on–spoils his story as it did so much else. Such an ending to such a romance is worse even than any blundering such as the commonplace inventor could be guilty of, for he would be in a low sense natural if he were but commonplace. We need not therefore be surprised to find Mr Gwynn thus writing:

> "The love scenes in *Weir of Hermiston* are almost unsurpassable; but the central interest of the story lies elsewhere – in the relations between father and son. Whatever the cause, the fact is clear that in the last years of his life Stevenson recognised in himself an ability to treat subjects which he had hitherto avoided, and was thus no longer under the necessity of detaching fragments from life. Before this, he had largely confined himself to the adventures of roving men where women had made no entrance; or, if he treated of a settled family group, the result was what we see in *The Master of Ballantrae*."

In a word, between this work and *Weir of Hermiston* we have the passage from mere youth to manhood, with its wider, calmer views, and its patience, inclusiveness, and mild, genial acceptance of types that before did not come, and could not by any effort of will be brought, within range or made to adhere consistently with what was already accepted and workable. He was less the egotist now and more the realist. He was not so prone to the high lights in which all seems overwrought, exaggerated; concerned really with effects of a more subdued order, if still the theme was a wee out of ordinary nature. Enough is left to prove that Stevenson's life-long devotion to his art anyway was on the point of being rewarded by such a success as he had always dreamt of: that in the man's nature there was power to conceive scenes of a tragic beauty and intensity unsurpassed in our prose literature, and to create characters not unworthy of his greatest predecessors. The blind stroke of fate had nothing to say to the lesson of his life, and though we deplore that he never completed his masterpieces, we may at least be thankful that time enough was given him to prove to his fellow-craftsmen, that such labour for the sake of art is not without art's peculiar reward – the triumph of successful execution.

CHAPTER XXIII – EDINBURGH REVIEWERS' DICTA INAPPLICABLE TO LATER WORK

From many different points of view discerning critics have celebrated the autobiographic vein – the self-revealing turn, the self-portraiture, the quaint, genial, yet really child-like egotistic and even dreamy element that lies like an amalgam, behind all Stevenson's work. Some have even said, that because of this, he will finally live by his essays and not by his stories. That is extreme, and is not critically based or justified, because, however true it may be up to a certain point, it is not true of Stevenson's quite latest fictions where we see a decided breaking through of the old limits, and an advance upon a new and a fresher and broader sphere of interest and character altogether. But these ideas set down truly enough at a certain date, or prior to a certain date, are wrong and falsely directed in view of Stevenson's latest work and what it promised. For instance, what a discerning and able writer in the *Edinburgh Review* of July 1895 said truly then was in great part utterly inapplicable to the whole of the work of the last years, for in it there was grasp, wide and deep, of new possibilities – promise of clear insight, discrimination, and contrast of character, as well as firm hold of new and great human interest under which the egotistic or autobiographic vein was submerged or weakened. The *Edinburgh Reviewer* wrote:

> "There was irresistible fascination in what it would be unfair to characterise as egotism, for it came natural to him to talk frankly and easily of himself. . . . He could never have dreamed, like Pepys, of locking up his confidence in a diary. From first to last, in inconsecutive essays, in the records of sentimental touring, in fiction and in verse, he has embodied the outer and the inner autobiography. He discourses – he prattles – he almost babbles about himself. He seems to have taken minute and habitual introspection for the chief study in his analysis of human nature, as a subject which was immediately in his reach, and would most surely serve his purpose. We suspect much of

the success of his novels was due to the fact that as he seized for a substructure on the scenery and situations which had impressed him forcibly, so in the characters of the most different types, there was always more or less of self-portraiture. The subtle touch, eminently and unmistakably realistic, gave life to what might otherwise have seemed a lay-figure. . . . He hesitated again and again as to his destination; and under mistakes, advice of friends, doubted his chances, as a story-writer, even after *Treasure Island* had enjoyed its special success. . . . We venture to think that, with his love of intellectual self-indulgence, had he found novel-writing really enjoyable, he would never have doubted at all. But there comes in the difference between him and Scott, whom he condemns for the slovenliness of hasty workmanship. Scott, in his best days, sat down to his desk and let the swift pen take its course in inspiration that seemed to come without an effort. Even when racked with pains, and groaning in agony, the intellectual machinery was still driven at a high pressure by something that resembled an irrepressible instinct. Stevenson can have had little or nothing of that inspiriting afflatus. He did his painstaking work conscientiously, thoughtfully; he erased, he revised, and he was hard to satisfy. In short, it was his weird—and he could not resist it—to set style and form before fire and spirit."

CHAPTER XXIV – MR HENLEY'S SPITEFUL PERVERSIONS

More unfortunate still, as disturbing and prejudicing a sane and true and disinterested view of Stevenson's claims, was that article of his erewhile "friend," Mr W. E. Henley, published on the appearance of the *Memoir* by Mr Graham Balfour, in the *Pall Mall Magazine*. It was well that Mr Henley there acknowledged frankly that he wrote under a keen sense of "grievance" – a most dangerous mood for the most soberly critical and self-restrained of men to write in, and that most certainly Mr W. E. Henley was not – and that he owned to having lost contact with, and recognition of the R. L. Stevenson who went to America in 1887, as he says, and never came back again. To do bare justice to Stevenson it is clear that knowledge of that later Stevenson was essential – essential whether it was calculated to deepen sympathy or the reverse. It goes without saying that the Louis he knew and hobnobbed with, and nursed near by the Old Bristo Port in Edinburgh could not be the same exactly as the Louis of Samoa and later years – to suppose so, or to expect so, would simply be to deny all room for growth and expansion. It is clear that the W. E. Henley of those days was not the same as the W. E. Henley who indited that article, and if growth and further insight are to be allowed to Mr Henley and be pleaded as his justification *cum* spite born of sense of grievance for such an onslaught, then clearly some allowance in the same direction must be made for Stevenson. One can hardly think that in his case old affection and friendship had been so completely submerged, under feelings of grievance and paltry pique, almost always bred of grievances dwelt on and nursed, which it is especially bad for men of genius to acknowledge, and to make a basis, as it were, for clearer knowledge, insight, and judgment. In other cases the pleading would simply amount to an immediate and complete arrest of judgment. Mr Henley throughout writes as though whilst he had changed, and changed in points most essential, his erewhile friend remained exactly where he was as to literary position and product – the Louis who went away in 1887 and never returned, had, as Mr W. E. Henley, most unfortunately for himself, would imply, retained the mastery, and the Louis who never came back had made no progress, had not added an inch, not to say a cubit, to his statue, while Mr Henley remained *in statu quo*, and was so only to be judged. It is an instance of the imperfect sympathy which Charles Lamb finely celebrated—only here it is acknowledged, and the "imperfect sympathy" pled as a ground for claiming the full insight which only sympathy can secure. If Mr Henley was fair to the Louis he knew and loved, it is clear that he was and could only be unjust to the Louis who went away in 1887 and never came back.

> "At bottom Stevenson was an excellent fellow. But he was of his essence what the French call *personnel*. He was, that is, incessantly and passionately interested in Stevenson. He could not be in the same room with a mirror but he must invite its confidences every time he passed it; to him there was nothing obvious in time and eternity, and the smallest of his discoveries, his most trivial apprehensions, were all by way of being revelations, and as revelations must be thrust upon the world; he was never so much in earnest, never so well pleased (this were he happy or wretched), never so irresistible as when he wrote about himself. *Withal, if he wanted a thing, he went after it with an entire contempt of consequences. For these, indeed, the Shorter Catechism was ever prepared to answer; so that whether he did well or ill, he was safe to come out unabashed and cheerful.*"

Notice here, how undiscerning the mentor becomes. The words put in "italics," unqualified as they are, would fit and admirably cover the character of the greatest criminal. They would do as they stand, for Wainwright, for Dr Dodd, for Deeming, for Neil Cream, for Canham Read, or for Dougal of Moat Farm fame. And then the touch that, in the Shorter Catechism, Stevenson would have found a cover or justification for it somehow! This comes of writing under a keen sense of grievance; and how could this be truly said of one who was "at bottom an excellent fellow." W. Henley's ethics are about as clear-obscure as is his reading of character. Listen to him once again—more directly on the literary point.

"To tell the truth, his books are none of mine; I mean that if I wanted reading, I do not go for it to the *Edinburgh Edition*. I am not interested in remarks about morals; in and out of letters. *I have lived a full and varied life*, and my opinions are my own. *So, if I crave the enchantment of romance, I ask it of bigger men than he, and of bigger books than his*: of *Esmond* (say) and *Great Expectations*, of *Redgauntlet* and *Old Mortality, of La Reine Margot* and *Bragelonne*, of *David Copperfield* and *A Tale of Two Cities*; while if good writing and some other things be in my appetite, are there not always Hazlitt and Lamb—to say nothing of that globe of miraculous continents; which is known to us as Shakespeare? There is his style, you will say, and it is a fact that it is rare, and *in the last* times better, because much simpler than in the first. But, after all, his style is so perfectly achieved that the achievement gets obvious: and when achievement gets obvious, is it not by way of becoming uninteresting? And is there not something to be said for the person who wrote that Stevenson always reminded him of a young man dressed the best he ever saw for the Burlington Arcade? [10] Stevenson's work in letters does not now take me much, and I decline to enter on the question of his immortality; since that, despite what any can say, will get itself settled soon or late, for all time. No—when I care to think of Stevenson it is not of R. L. Stevenson—R. L. Stevenson, the renowned, the accomplished—executing his difficult solo, but of the Lewis that I knew and loved, and wrought for, and worked with for so long. The successful man of letters does not greatly interest me. I read his careful prayers and pass on, with the certainty that, well as they read, they were not written for print. I learn of his nameless prodigalities, and recall some instances of conduct in another vein. I remember, rather, the unmarried and irresponsible Lewis; the friend, the comrade,

> the *charmeur*. Truly, that last word, French as it is, is the only one that is worthy of him. I shall ever remember him as that. The impression of his writings disappears; the impression of himself and his talk is ever a possession. . . . Forasmuch as he was primarily a talker, his printed works, like these of others after his kind, are but a sop for posterity. A last dying speech and confession (as it were) to show that not for nothing were they held rare fellows in their day."

Just a month or two before Mr Henley's self-revealing article appeared in the *Pall Mall Magazine*, Mr Chesterton, in the *Daily News*, with almost prophetic forecast, had said:

> "Mr Henley might write an excellent study of Stevenson, but it would only be of the Henleyish part of Stevenson, and it would show a distinct divergence from the finished portrait of Stevenson, which would be given by Professor Colvin."

And it were indeed hard to reconcile some things here with what Mr Henley set down of individual works many times in the *Scots and National Observer*, and elsewhere, and in literary judgments as in some other things there should, at least, be general consistency, else the search for an honest man in the late years would be yet harder than it was when Diogenes looked out from his tub!

Mr James Douglas, in the *Star*, in his half-playful and suggestive way, chose to put it as though he regarded the article in the *Pall Mall Magazine* as a hoax, perpetrated by some clever, unscrupulous writer, intent on provoking both Mr Henley and his friends, and Stevenson's friends and admirers. This called forth a letter from one signing himself "A Lover of R. L. Stevenson," which is so good that we must give it here.

A LITERARY HOAX.
TO THE EDITOR OF THE *STAR*.

> Sir—I fear that, despite the charitable scepticism of Mr Douglas, there is no doubt that Mr Henley is the perpetrator of the saddening Depreciation of

Stevenson which has been published over his name.

What openings there are for reprisals let Mr Henley's conscience tell him; but permit me to remind him of two or three things which R. L. Stevenson has written concerning W. E. Henley.

First this scene in the infirmary at Edinburgh:

"(Leslie) Stephen and I sat on a couple of chairs, and the poor fellow (Henley) sat up in his bed with his hair and beard all tangled, and talked as cheerfully as if he had been in a king's palace, or the great King's palace of the blue air. He has taught himself two languages since he has been lying there. *I shall try to be of use to him.*"

Secondly, this passage from Stevenson's dedication of *Virginibus Puerisque* to "My dear William Ernest Henley":

"These papers are like milestones on the wayside of my life; and as I look back in memory, there is hardly a stage of that distance but I see you present with advice, reproof, or praise. Meanwhile, many things have changed, you and I among the rest; but I hope that our sympathy, founded on the love of our art, and nourished by mutual assistance, shall survive these little revolutions, undiminished, and, with God's help, unite us to the end."

Thirdly, two scraps from letters from Stevenson to Henley, to show that the latter was not always a depreciator of R. L. Stevenson's work:

"1. I'm glad to think I owe you the review that pleased me best of all the reviews I ever had. . . . To live reading such reviews and die eating ortolans—sich is my aspiration.

> "2. Dear lad,—If there was any more praise in what you wrote, I think—(the editor who had pruned down Mr Henley's review of Stevenson's *Prince Otto*) has done us both a service; some of it stops my throat. . . . Whether (considering our intimate relations) you would not do better to refrain from reviewing me, I will leave to yourself."
>
> And, lastly, this extract from the very last of Stevenson's letters to Henley, published in the two volumes of *Letters*:
>
> "It is impossible to let your new volume pass in silence. I have not received the same thrill of poetry since G. M.'s *Joy of Earth* volume, and *Love in a Valley*; and I do not know that even that was so intimate and deep. . . . I thank you for the joy you have given me, and remain your old friend and present huge admirer, R. L. S."

It is difficult to decide on which side in this literary friendship lies the true modesty and magnanimity? I had rather be the author of the last message of R. L. Stevenson to W. E. Henley, than of the last words of W. E. Henley concerning R. L. Stevenson.

CHAPTER XXV – MR CHRISTIE MURRAY'S IMPRESSIONS

Mr Christie Murray, writing as "Merlin" in our handbook in the *Referee* at the time, thus disposed of some of the points just dealt with by us:

> "Here is libel on a large scale, and I have purposely refrained from approaching it until I could show my readers something of the spirit in which the whole attack is conceived. 'If he wanted a thing he went after it with an entire contempt for consequences. For these, indeed, the Shorter Catechist was ever prepared to answer; so that whether he did well or ill, he was safe to come out unabashed and cheerful.' Now if Mr Henley does not mean that for the very express picture of a rascal without a conscience he has been most strangely infelicitous in his choice of terms, and he is one of those who make so strong a profession of duty towards mere vocables that we are obliged to take him *au pied de la lettre*. A man who goes after whatever he wants with an entire contempt of consequences is a scoundrel, and the man who emerges from such an enterprise unabashed and cheerful, whatever his conduct may have been, and justifies himself on the principles of the Shorter Catechism, is a hypocrite to boot. This is not the report we have of Robert Louis Stevenson from most of those who knew him. It is a most grave and dreadful accusation, and it is not minimised by Mr Henley's acknowledgment that Stevenson was a good fellow. We all know the air of false candour which lends a disputant so much advantage in debate. In Victor Hugo's tremendous indictment of Napolion le Petit we remember the telling allowance for fine horsemanship. It spreads an air of impartiality over the most mordant of Hugo's pages. It is meant to do

that. An insignificant praise is meant to show how a whole Niagara of blame is poured on the victim of invective in all sincerity, and even with a touch of reluctance.

"Mr Henley, despite his absurdities of ''Tis' and 'it were,' is a fairly competent literary craftsman, and he is quite gifted enough to make a plain man's plain meaning an evident thing if he chose to do it. But if for the friend for whom 'first and last he did share' he can only show us the figure of one 'who was at bottom an excellent fellow,' and who had 'an entire contempt' for the consequences of his own acts, he presents a picture which can only purposely be obscured. . . .

"All I know of Robert Louis Stevenson I have learned from his books, and from one unexpected impromptu letter which he wrote to me years ago in friendly recognition of my own work. I add the testimonies of friends who may have been of less actual service to him than Mr Henley, but who surely loved him better and more lastingly. These do not represent him as the victim of an overweening personal vanity, nor as a person reckless of the consequences of his own acts, nor as a Pecksniff who consoled himself for moral failure out of the Shorter Catechism. The books and the friends amongst them show me an erratic yet lovable personality, a man of devotion and courage, a loyal, charming, and rather irresponsible person whose very slight faults were counter-balanced many times over by very solid virtues. . . .

"To put the thing flatly, it is not a heroism to cling to mere existence. The basest of us can do that. But it is a heroism to maintain an equable and unbroken cheerfulness in the face of death. For my own part, I never bowed at the literary shrine Mr Henley and his friends were at so great pains to

> rear. I am not disposed to think more loftily than I ever thought of their idol. But the Man—the Man was made of enduring valour and childlike charm, and these will keep him alive when his detractors are dead and buried."

As to the Christian name, it is notorious that he was christened Robert Lewis—the Lewis being after his maternal grandfather—Dr Lewis Balfour. Some attempt has been made to show that the Louis was adopted because so many cousins and relatives had also been so christened; but the most likely explanation I have ever heard was that his father changed the name to Louis, that there might be no chance through it of any notion of association with a very prominent noisy person of the name of Lewis, in Edinburgh, towards whom Thomas Stevenson felt dislike, if not positive animosity. Anyhow, it is clear from the entries in the register of pupils at the Edinburgh Academy, in the two years when Stevenson was there, that in early youth he was called Robert only; for in the school list for 1862 the name appears as Robert Stevenson, without the Lewis, while in the 1883 list it is given as Lewis Robert Stevenson. Clearly if in earlier years Stevenson was, in his family and elsewhere, called *Robert*, there could have then arisen no risk of confusion with any of his relatives who bore the name of Lewis; and all this goes to support the view which I have given above. Anyhow he ceased to be called Robert at home, and ceased in 1863 to be Robert on the Edinburgh Academy list, and became Lewis Robert. Whether my view is right or not, he was thenceforward called Louis in his family, and the name uniformly spelt Louis. What blame on Stevenson's part could be attached to this family determination it is hard to see—people are absolutely free to spell their names as they please, and the matter would not be worth a moment's attention, or the waste of one drop of ink, had not Mr Henley chosen to be very nasty about the name, and in the *Pall Mall Magazine* article persisted in printing it Lewis as though that were worthy of him and of it. That was not quite the unkindest cut of all, but it was as unkind as it was trumpery. Mr Christie Murray neatly set off the trumpery spite of this in the following passage:

> "Stevenson, it appears, according to his friend's judgment, was 'incessantly and passionately inter-

ested in Stevenson,' but most of us are incessantly and passionately interested in ourselves. 'He could not be in the same room with a mirror but he must invite its confidences every time he passed it.' I remember that George Sala, who was certainly under no illusion as to his own personal aspect, made public confession of an identical foible. Mr Henley may not have an equal affection for the looking-glass, but he is a very poor and unimaginative reader who does not see him gloating over the god-like proportions of the shadow he sends sprawling over his own page. I make free to say that a more self-conscious person than Mr Henley does not live. 'The best and most interesting part of Stevenson's life will never get written—even by me,' says Mr Henley.

"There is one curious little mark of animus, or one equally curious affectation—I do not profess to know which, and it is most probably a compound of the two—in Mr Henley's guardedly spiteful essay which asks for notice. The dead novelist signed his second name on his title-pages and his private correspondence 'Louis.' Mr Henley spells it 'Lewis.' Is this intended to say that Stevenson took an ornamenting liberty with his own baptismal appellation? If so, why not say the thing and have done with it? Or is it one of Mr Henley's wilful ridiculosities? It seems to stand for some sort of meaning, and to me, at least, it offers a jarring hint of small spitefulness which might go for nothing if it were not so well borne out by the general tone of Mr Henley's article. It is a small matter enough, God knows, but it is precisely because it is so very small that it irritates."

CHAPTER XXVI – HERO-VILLAINS

In truth, it must indeed be here repeated that Stevenson for the reason he himself gave about *Deacon Brodie* utterly fails in that healthy hatred of "fools and scoundrels" on which Carlyle somewhat incontinently dilated. Nor does he, as we have seen, draw the line between hero and villain of the piece, as he ought to have done; and, even for his own artistic purposes, has it too much all on one side, to express it simply. Art demands relief from any one phase of human nature, more especially of that phase, and even from what is morbid or exceptional. Admitting that such natures, say as Huish, the cockney, in the *Ebb-Tide* on the one side, and Prince Otto on the other are possible, it is yet absolutely demanded that they should not stand *alone,* but have their due complement and balance present in the piece also to deter and finally to tell on them in the action. If "a knave or villain," as George Eliot aptly said, is but a fool with a circumbendibus, this not only wants to be shown, but to have that definite human counterpart and corrective; and this not in any indirect and perfunctory way, but in a direct and effective sense. It is here that Stevenson fails – fails absolutely in most of his work, save the very latest – fails, as has been shown, in *The Master of Ballantrae,* as it were almost of perverse and set purpose, in lack of what one might call ethical decision which causes him to waver or seem to waver and wobble in his judgment of his characters or in his sympathy with them or for them. Thus he fails to give his readers the proper cue which was his duty both as man and artist to have given. The highest art and the lowest are indeed here at one in demanding moral poise, if we may call it so, that however crudely in the low, and however artistically and refinedly in the high, vice should not only not be set forth as absolutely triumphing, nor virtue as being absolutely, outwardly, and inwardly defeated. It is here the same in the melodrama of the transpontine theatre as in the tragedies of the Greek dramatists and Shakespeare. "The evening brings a' 'hame'" and the end ought to show something to satisfy the innate craving (for it is innate, thank Heaven! and low and high alike in moments of *elevated impression,* acknowledge it and bow to it) else there can scarce be true *dinouement* and the sense of any moral rectitude or law remain as felt or acknowledged in human nature or in the Universe itself.

Stevenson's toleration and constant sermonising in the essays—his desire to make us yield allowances all round is so far, it may be, there in place; but it will not work out in story or play, and declares the need for correction and limitation the moment that he essays artistic presentation—from the point of view of art he lacks at once artistic clearness and decision, and from the point of view of morality seems utterly loose and confusing. His artistic quality here rests wholly in his style—mere style, and he is, alas! a castaway as regards discernment and reading of human nature in its deepest demands and laws. Herein lies the false strain that has spoiled much of his earlier work, which renders really superficial and confusing and undramatic his professedly dramatic work—which never will and never can commend the hearty suffrages of a mixed and various theatrical audience in violating the very first rule of the theatre, and of dramatic creation.

From another point of view this is my answer to Mr Pinero in regard to the failure of Stevenson to command theatrical success. He confuses and so far misdirects the sympathies in issues which strictly are at once moral and dramatic.

I am absolutely at one with Mr Baildon, though I reach my results from somewhat different grounds from what he does, when he says this about *Beau Austin*, and the reason of its failure—complete failure—on the stage:

> "I confess I should have liked immensely to have seen [? to see] this piece on the boards; for only then could one be quite sure whether it could be made convincing to an audience and carry their sympathies in the way the author intended. Yet the fact that *Beau Austin*, in spite of being 'put on' by so eminent an actor-manager as Mr Beerbohm Tree, was no great success on the stage, is a fair proof that the piece lacked some of the essentials, good or bad, of dramatic success. Now a drama, like a picture or a musical composition, must have a certain unity of key and tone. You can, indeed,

mingle comedy with tragedy as an interlude or relief from the strain and stress of the serious interest of the piece. But you cannot reverse the process and mingle tragedy with comedy. Once touch the fine spun-silk of the pretty fire-balloon of comedy with the tragic dagger, and it falls to earth a shrivelled nothing. And the reason that no melodrama can be great art is just that it is a compromise between tragedy and comedy, a mixture of tragedy with comedy and not comedy with tragedy. So in drama, the middle course, proverbially the safest, is in reality the most dangerous. Now I maintain that in *Beau Austin* we have an element of tragedy. The betrayal of a beautiful, pure and noble-minded woman is surely at once the basest act a man can be capable of, and a more tragic event than death itself to the woman. Richardson, in *Clarissa Harlowe*, is well aware of this, and is perfectly right in making his *dinouement* tragic. Stevenson, on the other hand, patches up the matter into a rather tame comedy. It is even much tamer than it would have been in the case of Lovelace and Clarissa Harlowe; for Lovelace is a strong character, a man who could have been put through some crucial atonement, and come out purged and ennobled. But Beau Austin we feel is but a frip. He endures a few minutes of sharp humiliation, it is true, but to the spectator this cannot but seem a very insufficient expiation, not only of the wrong he had done one woman, but of the indefinite number of wrongs he had done others. He is at once the villain and the hero of the piece, and in the narrow limits of a brief comedy this transformation cannot be convincingly effected. Wrongly or rightly, a theatrical audience, like the spectators of a trial, demand a definite verdict and sentence, and no play can satisfy which does not reasonably meet this demand. And this arises not from any merely Christian

> prudery or Puritanism, for it is as true for Greek tragedy and other high forms of dramatic art."

The transformation of villain into hero, if possible at all, could only be convincingly effected in a piece of wide scope, where there was room for working out the effect of some great shock, upheaval of the nature, change due to deep and unprecedented experiences—religious conversion, witnessing of sudden death, providential rescue from great peril of death, or circumstance of that kind; but to be effective and convincing it needs to be marked and *fully justified* in some such way; and no cleverness in the writer will absolve him from deference to this great law in serious work for presentation on the stage; if mere farces or little comedies may seem sometimes to contravene it, yet this—even this—is only in appearance.

True, it is not the dramatists part *of himself* to condemn, or to approve, or praise: he has to present, and to present various characters faithfully in their relation to each other, and their effect upon each other. But the moral element cannot be expunged or set lightly aside because it is closely involved in the very working out and presentation of these relations, and the effect upon each other. Character is vital. And character, if it tells in life, in influence and affection, must be made to tell directly also in the drama. There is no escape from this—none; the dramatist is lopsided if he tries to ignore it; he is a monster if he is wholly blind to it—like the poet in *In Memoriam,* "Without a conscience or an aim." Mr Henley, in his notorious, all too confessional, and yet rather affected article on Stevenson in the *Pall Mall Magazine*, has a remark which I confess astonished me—a remark I could never forget as coming from him. He said that he "had lived a very full and varied life, and had no interest in remarks about morals." "Remarks about morals" are, nevertheless, in essence, the pith of all the books to which he referred, as those to which he turned in preference to the *Edinburgh Edition* of R. L. Stevenson's works. The moral element is implicit in the drama, and it is implicit there because it is implicit in life itself, or so the great commonsense conceives it and demands it. What we might call the asides proper of the drama, are "remarks about morals," nothing else—the chorus in the Greek tragedy gathered up "remarks about morals" as near as might be to the "remarks about morals" in the streets of that day, only shaped to a certain artistic consistency. Shakespeare is rich in "remarks about morals," often coming near, indeed, to personal utterance, and this not only when Polonius addresses his son before his going forth on his travels. Mr Henley here only too plainly confessed, indeed, to lack of that conviction and insight which, had he but possessed them, might have done a little to relieve *Beau Austin* and the other plays in which he collaborated with R. L. Stevenson, from their besetting and fatal weakness. The two youths, alas! thought they could be grandly original by despising, or worse, contemning "remarks about morals" in the loftier as in the lower sense. To "live a full and varied life," if the experience derived from it is to have expression in the drama, is only to have the richer resource in "remarks about morals." If this is perverted under any self-conscious notion of doing something spick-and-span new in the way of character and plot, alien to all the old conceptions, then we know our writers set themselves boldly at loggerheads with certain old-fashioned and yet older new-fashioned laws, which forbid the violation of certain common demands of the ordinary nature and common-sense; and for the lack of this, as said already, no cleverness, no resource, no style or graft, will any way make up. So long as this is tried, with whatever concentration of mind and purpose, failure is yet inevitable, and the more inevitable the more concentration and less of humorous by-play, because genius itself, if it despises the general moral sentiment and instinct for moral proportion—an ethnic reward and punishment, so to say—is all astray, working outside the line; and this, if Mr Pinero will kindly excuse me, is the secret of the failure of these plays, and not want of concentration, etc., in the sense he meant, or as he has put it.

Stevenson rather affected what he called "tail-foremost morality," a kind of inversion in the field of morals, as De Quincey mixed it up with tail-foremost humour in *Murder as a Fine Art*, etc., etc., but for all such perversions as these the stage is a grand test and corrector, and such perversions, and not "remarks about morals," are most strictly prohibited there. Perverted subtleties of the sort Stevenson in earlier times especially much affected are not only amiss but ruinous on the stage; and what genius itself would maybe sanction, common-sense must reject and rigidly cut away. Final success and triumph come largely by *this* kind of condensation and concentration, and the stern and severe lopping off of the indulgence of the *egotistical* genius, which is human discipline, and the best exponent of the doctrine of unity also. This is the straight and the narrow way along which genius, if it walk but faithfully, sows as it goes in the dramatic pathway all the flowers of human passion, hope, love, terror, and triumph.

I find it advisable, if not needful, here to reinforce my own impressions, at some points, by another quotation from Mr Baildon, if he will allow me, in which Stevenson's dependence in certain respects on the dream-faculty is emphasised, and to it is traced a certain tendency to a moral callousness or indifference which is one of the things in which the waking Stevenson transparently suffered now and then invasions from the dream-Stevenson—the result, a kind of spot, as we may call it, on the eye of the moral sense; it is a small spot; but we know how a very small object held close before the eye will wholly shut out the most lovely natural prospects, interposing distressful phantasmagoria, due to the strained and, for the time, morbid condition of the organ itself. So, it must be confessed, it is to a great extent here.

But listen to Mr Baildon:

"In *A Chapter on Dreams*, Stevenson confesses his indebtedness to this still mysterious agency. From a child he had been a great and vivid dreamer, his dreams often taking such frightful shape that he used to awake 'clinging in terror to the bedpost.' Later in life his dreams continued to be frequent and vivid, but less terrifying in character and more continuous and systematic. 'The Brownies,' as he picturesquely names that 'sub-conscious imagination,' as the scientist would call it, that works with such surprising freedom and ingenuity in our dreams, became, as it were, *collaborateurs* in his work of authorship. He declares that they invented plots and even elaborated whole novels, and that, not in a single night or single dream, but continuously, and from one night to another, like a story in serial parts. Long before this essay was written or published, I had been struck by this phantasmal dream-like quality in some of Stevenson's works, which I was puzzled to account for, until I read this extraordinary explanation, for explanation it undoubtedly affords. Anything imagined in a dream would have a tendency, when retold, to retain something of its dream-like character, and I have on doubt one could trace in many instances and distinguish the dreaming and the waking Stevenson, though in others they may be blended beyond recognition. The trouble with the Brownies or the dream-Stevenson *was his or their want of moral sense,* so that they sometimes presented the waking author with plots which he could not make use of. Of this Stevenson gives an instance in which a complete story of marked ingenuity is vetoed through the moral impossibility of its presentment by a writer so scrupulous (and in some directions he is extremely scrupulous) as Stevenson was. But Stevenson admits that his most famous story, *The Strange Case of Dr Jekyll and Mr Hyde,* was not only suggested by a dream, but that some of the most important and most criticised points, such as the matter of the powder, were taken direct from the dream. It had been extremely instructive and interesting had he gone more into detail and mentioned some of the other stories into which the dream-element entered largely and pointed out its influence, and would have given us a better clue than we have or now ever can have.

"Even in *The Suicide Club* and the *Rajah's Diamond,* I seem to feel strongly the presence of the dream-Stevenson. . . . *At certain points one feels conscious of a certain moral callousness, such as marks the dream state, as in the murder of Colonel Geraldine's brother, the horror of which never seems to come fully home to us.* But let no one suppose these stories are lacking in vividness and in strangely realistic detail; for this is of the very nature of dreaming at its height. . . . While the *dramatis personf* play their parts with the utmost spirit while the story proceeds, they do not, as the past creations do, seem to survi-ve this first contact and live in our minds. This is particularly true of the women. They are well drawn, and play the assigned parts well enough, but they do not, as a rule, make a place for themselves eit-her in our hearts or memories. If there is an exception it is Elvira, in *Providence and the Guitar;* but we remember her chiefly by the one picture of her falling asleep, after the misadventures of the night, at the supper-table, with her head on her husband's shoulder, and her hand locked in his with instinctive, almost unconscious tender-ness."

CHAPTER XXVII – MR G. MOORE, MR MARRIOTT WATSON AND OTHERS

From our point of view it will therefore be seen that we could not have read Mr George Moore's wonderfully uncritical and misdirected diatribe against Stevenson in *The Daily Chronicle* of 24th April 1897, without amusement, if not without laughter – indeed, we confess we may here quote Shakespeare's words, we "laughed so consumedly" that, unless for Mr Moore's high position and his assured self-confidence, we should not trust ourselves to refer to it, not to speak of writing about it. It was a review of *The Secret Rose* by W. B. Yeats, but it passed after one single touch to belittling abuse of Stevenson – an abuse that was justified the more, in Mr Moore's idea, because Stevenson was dead. Had he been alive he might have had something to say to it, in the way, at least, of fable and moral. And when towards the close Mr Moore again quotes from Mr Yeats, it is still "harping on my daughter" to undo Stevenson, as though a rat was behind the arras, as in *Hamlet*. "Stevenson," says he, "is the leader of these countless writers who perceive nothing but the visible world," and these are antagonistic to the great literature, of which Mr Yeats's *Secret Rose* is a survival or a renaissance, a literature whose watchword should be Mr Yeats's significant phrase, "When one looks into the darkness there is always something there." No doubt Mr Yeats's product all along the line ranks with the great literature – unlike Homer, according to Mr Moore, he never nods, though in the light of great literature, poor Stevenson is always at his noddings, and more than that, in the words of Leland's Hans Breitmann, he has "nodings on." He is poor, naked, miserable – a mere pretender – and has no share in the makings of great literature. Mr Moore has stripped him to the skin, and leaves him to the mercy of rain and storm, like Lear, though Lear had a solid ground to go on in self-aid, which Stevenson had not; he had daughters, and one of them was Cordelia, after all. This comes of painting all boldly in black and white: Mr Yeats is white, R. L. Stevenson is black, and I am sure neither one nor other, because simply of their self-devotion to their art, could have subscribed heartily to Mr Moore's black art and white art theory. Mr Yeats is hardly the truest modern Celtic artist I take him for, if he can fully subscribe to all this.

Mr Marriott Watson has a little unadvisedly, in my view, too like ambition, fallen on 'tother side, and celebrated Stevenson as the master of the horrifying. [11] He even finds the *Ebb-Tide*, and Huish, the cockney, in it richly illustrative and grand. "There never was a more magnificent cad in literature, and never a more foul-hearted little ruffian. His picture glitters (!) with life, and when he curls up on the island beach with the bullet in his body, amid the flames of the vitriol he had intended for another, the reader's shudder conveys something also, even (!) of regret."

And well it may! Individual taste and opinion are but individual taste and opinion, but the *Ebb-Tide* and the cockney I should be inclined to cite as a specimen of Stevenson's all too facile make-believe, in which there is too definite a machinery set agoing for horrors for the horrors to be quite genuine. The process is often too forced with Stevenson, and the incidents too much of the manufactured order, for the triumph of that simplicity which is of inspiration and unassailable. Here Stevenson, alas! all too often, *pace* Mr Marriott Watson, treads on the skirts of E. A. Poe, and that in his least composed and elevated artistic moments. And though, it is true, that "genius will not follow rules laid down by desultory critics," yet when it is averred that "this piece of work fulfils Aristotle's definition of true tragedy, in accomplishing upon the reader a certain purification of the emotions by means of terror and pity," expectations will be raised in many of the new generation, doomed in the cases of the more sensitive and discerning, at all events, not to be gratified. There is a distinction, very bold and very essential, between melodrama, however carefully worked and staged, and that tragedy to which Aristotle was there referring. Stevenson's "horrifying," to my mind, too often touches the trying borders of melodrama, and nowhere more so than in the very forced and unequal *Ebb-Tide*, which, with its rather doubtful moral and forced incident when it is good, seems merely to borrow from what had gone before, if not a very little even from some of what came after. No service is done to an author like Stevenson by fatefully praising him for precisely the wrong thing.

> "Romance attracted Stevenson, at least during the earlier part of his life, as a lodestone attracts the magnet. To romance he brought the highest gifts, and he has left us not only essays of delicate humour" (should this not be "essays *full of" or* "characterised by"?) "and sensitive imagination, but stories also which thrill with the realities of life, which are faithful pictures of the times and tempers he dealt with, and which, I firmly believe, will live so" (should it not be "as"?) "long as our noble English language."

Mr Marriott Watson sees very clearly in some things; but occasionally he misses the point. The problem is here raised how two honest, far-seeing critics could see so very differently on so simple a subject.

Mr Baildon says about the *Ebb-Tide*:

> "I can compare his next book, the *Ebb-Tide* (in collaboration with Osbourne) to little better than a mud-bath, for we find ourselves, as it were, unrelieved by dredging among the scum and dregs of humanity, the 'white trash' of the Pacific. Here we have Stevenson's masterly but utterly revolting incarnation of the lowest, vilest, vulgarest villainy in the cockney, Huish. Stevenson's other villains shock us by their cruel and wicked conduct; but there is a kind of fallen satanic glory about them, some shining threads of possible virtue. They might have been good, even great in goodness, but for the malady of not wanting. But Huish is a creature hatched in slime, his soul has no true humanity: it is squat and toad-like, and can only spit venom. . . . He himself felt a sort of revulsive aftersickness for the story, and calls it in one passage of his *Vailima Letters* 'the ever-to-be-execrated *Ebb-Tide*' (pp. 178 and 184). . . . He repented of it like a debauch, and, as with some men after a debauch, felt cleared and strengthened instead of wrecked.

> So, after what in one sense was his lowest plunge, Stevenson rose to the greatest height. That is the tribute to his virtue and strength indeed, but it does not change the character of the *Ebb-Tide* as 'the ever-to-be-execrated.'"

Mr Baildon truly says (p. 49):

> "The curious point is that Stevenson's own great fault, that tendency to what has been called the 'Twopence-coloured' style, is always at its worst in books over which he collaborated."

"Verax," in one of his "Occasional Papers" in the *Daily News* on "The Average Reader" has this passage:

> "We should not object to a writer who could repeat Barrie in *A Window in Thrums*, nor to one who would paint a scene as Louis Stevenson paints Attwater alone on his South Sea island, the approach of the pirates to the harbour, and their subsequent reception and fate. All these are surely specimens of brilliant writing, and they are brilliant because, in the first place, they give truth. The events described must, in the supposed circumstances, and with the given characters, have happened in the way stated. Only in none of the specimens have we a mere photograph of the outside of what took place. We have great pictures by genius of the—to the prosaic eye—invisible realities, as well as of the outward form of the actions. We behold and are made to feel the solemnity, the wildness, the pathos, the earnestness, the agony, the pity, the moral squalor, the grotesque fun, the delicate and minute beauty, the natural loveliness and loneliness, the quiet desperate bravery, or whatever else any of these wonderful pictures disclose to our view. Had we been lookers-on, we, the average readers, could not have seen these qualities for ourselves. But they are there, and ge-

> nius enables us to see them. Genius makes truth shine.
>
> "Is it not, therefore, probable that the brilliancy which we average readers do not want, and only laugh at when we get it, is something altogether different? I think I know what it is. It is an attempt to describe with words without thoughts, an effort to make readers see something the writer has never seen himself in his mind's eye. He has no revelation, no vision, nothing to disclose, and to produce an impression uses words, words, words, makes daub, daub, daub, without any definite purpose, and certainly without any real, or artistic, or definite effect. To describe, one must first of all see, and if we see anything the description of it will, as far as it is in us, come as effortless and natural as the leaves on trees, or as 'the tender greening of April meadows.' I, therefore, more than suspect that the brilliancy which the average reader laughs at is not brilliancy. A pot of flaming red paint thrown at a canvas does not make a picture."

Now there is vision for outward picture or separate incident, which may exist quite apart from what may be called moral, spiritual, or even loftily imaginative conception, at once commanding unity and commanding it. There can be no doubt of Stevenson's power in the former line—the earliest as the latest of his works are witnesses to it. *The Master of Ballantrae* abounds in picture and incident and dramatic situations and touches; but it lacks true unity, and the reason simply is given by Stevenson himself—that the "ending shames, perhaps degrades, the beginning," as it is in the *Ebb-Tide*, with the cockney Huish, "execrable." "We have great pictures by genius of the—to the prosaic eye—invisible realities, as well as the outward form of the action." True, but the "invisible realities" form that from which true unity is derived, else their partial presence but makes the whole the more incomplete and lopsided, if not indeed, top-heavy, from light weight beneath; and it is in the unity derived from this higher pervading, yet not too assertive "invisible reality," that Stevenson most often fails, and is, in his own words, "execrable"; the ending shaming, if not degrading, the beginning—"and without the true sense of pleasurableness; and therefore really imperfect *in essence*." Ah, it is to be feared that Stevenson, viewing it in retrospect, was a far truer critic of his own work, than many or most of his all too effusive and admiring critics—from Lord Rosebery to Mr Marriott Watson.

Amid the too extreme deliverances of detractors and especially of erewhile friends, become detractors or panegyrists, who disturb judgment by overzeal, which is often but half-blindness, it is pleasant to come on one who bears the balances in his hand, and will report faithfully as he has seen and felt, neither more nor less than what he holds is true. Mr Andrew Lang wrote an article in the *Morning Post* of 16th December 1901, under the title "Literary Quarrels," in which, as I think, he fulfilled his part in midst of the talk about Mr Henley's regrettable attack on Stevenson.

> "Without defending the character of a friend whom even now I almost daily miss, as that character was displayed in circumstances unknown to me, I think that I ought to speak of him as I found him. Perhaps our sympathy was mainly intellectual. Constantly do those who knew him desire to turn to him, to communicate with him, to share with him the pleasure of some idea, some little discovery about men or things in which he would have taken pleasure, increasing our own by the gaiety of his enjoyment, the brilliance of his appreciation. We may say, as Scott said at the grave of John Ballantyne, that he has taken with him half the sunlight out of our lives. That he was sympathetic and interested in the work of others (which I understand has been denied) I have reason to know. His work and mine lay far apart: mine, I think, we never discussed, I did not expect it to interest him. But in a fragmentary manuscript of his after his death I found the unlooked for and touching evidence of his kindness. Again, he once wrote to me from Samoa about the work of a friend of mine whom he had never met. His re-

marks were ideally judicious, a model of serviceable criticism. I found him chivalrous as an honest boy; brave, with an indomitable gaiety of courage; on the point of honour, a Sydney or a Bayard (so he seemed to me); that he was open-handed I have reason to believe; he took life 'with a frolic welcome.' That he was self-conscious, and saw himself as it were, from without; that he was fond of attitude (like his own brave admirals) he himself knew well, and I doubt not that he would laugh at himself and his habit of 'playing at' things after the fashion of childhood. Genius is the survival into maturity of the inspiration of childhood, and Stevenson is not the only genius who has retained from childhood something more than its inspiration. Other examples readily occur to the memory – in one way Byron, in another Tennyson. None of us is perfect: I do not want to erect an immaculate clay-cold image of a man, in marble or in sugar-candy. But I will say that I do not remember ever to have heard Mr Stevenson utter a word against any mortal, friend or foe. Even in a case where he had, or believed himself to have, received some wrong, his comment was merely humorous. Especially when very young, his dislike of respectability and of the *bourgeois* (a literary tradition) led him to show a kind of contempt for virtues which, though certainly respectable, are no less certainly virtuous. He was then more or less seduced by the Bohemian legend, but he was intolerant of the fudge about the rights and privileges of genius. A man's first business, he thought, was 'keep his end up' by his work. If, what he reckoned his inspired work would not serve, then by something else. Of many virtues he was an ensample and an inspiring force. One foible I admit: the tendency to inopportune benevolence. Mr Graham Balfour says that if he fell into ill terms with a man he would try to do him good by stealth. Though he had seen much of the world and of men, this practice showed an invincible ignorance of mankind. It is improbable, on the doctrine of chances, that he was always in the wrong; and it is probable, as he was human, that he always thought himself in the right. But as the other party to the misunderstanding, being also human, would necessarily think himself in the right, such secret benefits would be, as Sophocles says, 'the gifts of foeman and unprofitable.' The secret would leak out, the benefits would be rejected, the misunderstanding would be embittered. This reminds me of an anecdote which is not given in Mr Graham Balfour's biography. As a little delicate, lonely boy in Edinburgh, Mr Stevenson read a book called *Ministering Children*. I have a faint recollection of this work concerning a small Lord and Lady Bountiful. Children, we know, like to 'play at' the events and characters they have read about, and the boy wanted to play at being a ministering child. He 'scanned his whole horizon' for somebody to play with, and thought he had found his playmate. From the window he observed street boys (in Scots 'keelies') enjoying themselves. But one child was out of the sports, a little lame fellow, the son of a baker. Here was a chance! After some misgivings Louis hardened his heart, put on his cap, walked out—a refined little figure—approached the object of his sympathy, and said, 'Will you let me play with you?' 'Go to hell!' said the democratic offspring of the baker. This lesson against doing good by stealth to persons of unknown or hostile disposition was, it seems, thrown away. Such endeavours are apt to be misconstrued."

CHAPTER XXVIII – UNEXPECTED COMBINATIONS

The complete artist should not be mystical-moralist any more than the man who "perceives only the visible world" – he should not engage himself with problems in the direct sense any more than he should blind himself to their effect upon others, whom he should study, and under certain conditions represent, though he should not commit himself to any form of zealot faith, yet should he not be, as Lord Tennyson puts it in the Palace of Art:

> "As God holding no form of creed,
> But contemplating all,"

because his power lies in the broadness of his humanity touched to fine issues whenever there is the seal at once of truth, reality, and passion, and the tragedy bred of their contact and conflict.

All these things are to him real and clamant in the measure that they aid appeal to heart and emotion – in the measure that they may, in his hands, be made to tell for sympathy and general effect. He creates an atmosphere in which each and all may be seen the more effectively, but never seen alone or separate, but only in strict relation to each other that they may heighten the sense of some supreme controlling power in the destinies of men, which with the ancients was figured as Fate, and for which the moderns have hardly yet found an enduring and exhaustive name. Character revealed in reference to that, is the ideal and the aim of all high creative art. Stevenson's narrowness, allied to a quaint and occasionally just a wee pedantic finickiness, as we may call it – an over-elaborate, almost tricky play with mere words and phrases, was in so far alien to the very highest – he was too often like a man magnetised and moving at the dictates of some outside influence rather than according to his own freewill and as he would.

Action in creative literary art is a *sine qub non*; keeping all the characters and parts in unison, that a true *dinouement*, determined by their own tendencies and temperaments, may appear; dialogue and all asides, if we may call them so, being supererogatory and weak really unless they aid this and are constantly contributory to it. Egotistical predeterminations, however artfully intruded, are, alien to the full result, the unity which is finally craved: Stevenson fails, when he does fail, distinctly from excess of egotistic regards; he is, as Henley has said, in the French sense, too *personnel*, and cannot escape from it. And though these personal regards are exceedingly interesting and indeed fascinating from the point of view of autobiographical study, they are, and cannot but be, a drawback on fiction or the disinterested revelation of life and reality. Instead, therefore, of "the visible world," as the only thing seen, Stevenson's defect is, that between it and him lies a cloud strictly self-projected, like breath on a mirror, which dims the lines of reality and confuses the character marks, in fact melting them into each other; and in his sympathetic regards, causing them all to become too much alike. Scott had more of the power of healthy self-withdrawal, creating more of a free atmosphere, in which his characters could freely move—though in this, it must be confessed, he failed far more with women than with men. The very defects poor Carlyle found in Scott, and for which he dealt so severely with him, as sounding no depth, are really the basis of his strength, precisely as the absence of them were the defects of Goethe, who invariably ran his characters finally into the mere moods of his own mind and the mould of his errant philosophy, so that they became merely erratic symbols without hold in the common sympathy. Whether *Walverwandschaften*, *Wilhelm Meister*, or *Faust*, it is still the same—the company before all is done are translated into misty shapes that he actually needs to label for our identification and for his own. Even Mr G. H. Lewes saw this and could not help declaring his own lack of interest in the latter parts of Goethe's greatest efforts. Stevenson, too, tends to run his characters into symbols—his moralist-fabulist determinations are too much for him—he would translate them into a kind of chessmen, moved or moving on a board. The essence of romance strictly is, that as the characters will not submit themselves to the check of reality, the romancer may consciously, if it suits him, touch them at any point with the magic wand of symbol, and if he finds a consistency in mere fanciful invention it is enough. Tieck's *Phantasus* and George MacDonald's *Phantastes* are ready instances illustrative of this. But it is very different with the story of real life, where there is a definite check in the common-sense and knowledge of the reader, and where the highest victory always lies in drawing from the reader the admission—"that is life—life exactly as I have seen and known it. Though I could never have put it so, still it only realises my own conception and observation. That is something lovingly remembered and re-presented, and this master makes me lovingly remember too, though 'twas his to represent and reproduce with such vigor, vividness and truth that he carried me with him, exactly as though I had been looking on real men and women playing their part or their game in the great world."

Mr Zangwill, in his own style, wrote:

> "He seeks to combine the novel of character with the novel of adventure; to develop character through romantic action, and to bring out your hero at the end of the episode, not the fixed character he was at the beginning, as is the way of adventure books, but a modified creature. . . . It is his essays and his personality, rather than his novels, that will count with posterity. On the whole, a great provincial writer. Whether he has that inherent grip which makes a man's provinciality the very source of his strength . . . only the centuries can show.

The romanticist to the end pursued Stevenson—he could not, wholly or at once, shake off the bonds in which he had bound himself to his first love, and it was the romanticist crossed by the casuist, and the mystic—Dr Jekyll and Mr Hyde, Markheim and Will of the Mill, insisted on his acknowledging them in his work up to the end. *The modified creature* at the end of Mr Zangwill was modified too directly by the egotistic element as well as through the romantic action, and this point missed the great defect was missed, and Mr Zangwill spoke only in generals.

M. Schwob, after having related how unreal a real sheep's heart looked when introduced on the end of Giovanni's dagger in a French performance of John Ford's *Annabella and Giovanni*, and how at the next performance the audience was duly thrilled when Annabella's bleeding heart, made of a bit of red flannel, was borne upon the stage, goes on to say significantly:

"Il me semble que les personnages de Stevenson ont justement cette esphce de rialisme irrial. La large figure luisante de Long John, la couleur bljme du crbne de Thevenin Pensete s'attachent ` la mimoire de nos yeux en vertue de leur irrialiti mjme. Ce sont des fanttmes de la viriti, hallucinants comme de vrais fanttmes. Notez en passant que les traits de John Silver hallucinent Jim Hawkins, et que Frangois Villon est hanti par l'aspect de Thevenin Pensete."

Perhaps the most notable fact arising here, and one that well deserves celebration, is this, that Stevenson's development towards a broader and more natural creation was coincident with a definite return on the religious views which had so powerfully prevailed with his father—a circumstance which it is to be feared did not, any more than some other changes in him, at all commend itself to Mr Henley, though he had deliberately dubbed him even in the times of nursing nigh to the Old Bristo Port in Edinburgh—something of "Shorter Catechist." Anyway Miss Simpson deliberately wrote:

"Mr Henley takes exception to Stevenson's later phase in life—what he calls his 'Shorter Catechism phase.' It should be remembered that Mr Henley is not a Scotsman, and in some things has little sympathy with Scotch characteristics. Stevenson, in his Samoan days, harked back to the teaching of his youth; the tenets of the Shorter Catechism, which his mother and nurse had dinned into his head, were not forgotten. Mr Henley knew him best, as Stevenson says in the preface to *Virginibus Puerisque* dedicated to Henley, 'when he lived his life at twenty-five.' In these days he had [in some degree] forgotten about the Shorter Catechism, but the 'solemn pause' between Saturday and Monday came back in full force to R. L. Stevenson in Samoa."

Now to me that is a most suggestive and significant fact. It will be the business of future critics to show in how far such falling back would of necessity modify what Mr Baildon has set down as his corner-stone of morality, and how far it was bound to modify the atmosphere – the purely egotistic, hedonistic, and artistic atmosphere, in which, in his earlier life as a novelist, at all events, he had been, on the whole, for long whiles content to work.

CHAPTER XXIX – LOVE OF VAGABONDS

What is very remarkable in Stevenson is that a man who was so much the dreamer of dreams – the mystic moralist, the constant questioner and speculator on human destiny and human perversity, and the riddles that arise on the search for the threads of motive and incentives to human action – moreover, a man, who constantly suffered from one of the most trying and weakening forms of ill-health – should have been so full-blooded, as it were, so keen for contact with all forms of human life and character, what is called the rougher and coarser being by no means excluded. Not only this: he was himself a rover – seeking daily adventure and contact with men and women of alien habit and taste and liking. His patience is supported by his humour. He was a bit of a vagabond in the good sense of the word, and always going round in search of "honest men," like Diogenes, and with no tub to retire into or the desire for it. He thus on this side touches the Chaucers and their kindred, as well as the Spensers and Dantes and their often illusive *confrhres*. His voyage as a steerage passenger across the Atlantic is only one out of a whole chapter of such episodes, and is more significant and characteristic even than the *Travels with a Donkey in the Cevennes* or the *Inland Voyage*. These might be ranked with the "Sentimental Journeys" that have sometimes been the fashion – that was truly of a prosaic and risky order. The appeal thus made to an element deep in the English nature will do much to keep his memory green in the hearts that could not rise to appreciation of his style and literary gifts at all. He loves the roadways and the by-ways, and those to be met with there – like him in this, though unlike him in most else. The love of the roadsides and the greenwood – and the queer miscellany of life there unfolded and ever changing – a kind of gipsy-like longing for the tent and familiar contact with nature and rude human-nature in the open dates from beyond Chaucer, and remains and will have gratification – the longing for novelty and all the accidents, as it were, of pilgrimage and rude social travel. You see it bubble up, like a true and new nature-spring, through all the surface coatings of culture and artificiality, in Stevenson. He anew, without pretence, enlivens it – makes it first a part of himself, and then a part of literature once more. Listen to him, as he sincerely sings this passion for the pilgrimage—or the modern phase of it—innocent vagabond roving:

> "Give to me the life I love,
> Let the lave go by me;
> Give the jolly heaven above,
> And the by-way nigh me:
> Bed in the bush, with stars to see;
> Bread I dip in the river—
> Here's the life for a man like me,
> Here's the life for ever. . . .
>
> "Let the blow fall soon or late;
> Let what will be o'er me;
> Give the face of earth around
> And the road before me.
> Health I ask not, hope nor love,
> Nor a friend to know me:
> All I ask the heaven above,
> And the road below me."

True; this is put in the mouth of another, but Stevenson could not have so voiced it, had he not been the born rover that he was, with longing for the roadside, the high hills, and forests and newcomers and varied miscellaneous company. Here he does more directly speak in his own person and quite to the same effect:

> "I will make you brooches and toys for your delight
> Of bird song at morning, and star shine at night,
> I will make a palace fit for you and me,
> Of green days in forests and blue days at sea.
>
> "I will make my kitchen, and you shall keep your room,
> Where white flows the river, and bright blows the broom,
> And you shall wash your linen and keep your body white,
> In rainfall at morning and dew-fall at night.

"And this shall be for music when no one else is near,
The fine song for singing, the rare song to hear!
That only I remember, that only you admire,
Of the broad road that stretches, and the roadside fire."

Here Stevenson, though original in his vein and way, but follows a great and gracious company in which Fielding and Sterne and so many others stand as pleasant proctors. Scott and Dickens have each in their way essayed it, and made much of it beyond what mere sentiment would have reached. *Pickwick* itself—and we must always regard Dickens as having himself gone already over every bit of road, described every nook and corner, and tried every resource—is a vagrant fellow, in a group of erratic and most quaint wanderers or pilgrims. This is but a return phase of it; Vincent Crummles and Mrs Crummles and the "Infant Phenomenon," yet another. The whole interest lies in the roadways, and the little inns, and the odd and unexpected *rencontres* with oddly-assorted fellows there experienced: glimpses of grim or grimy, or forbidding, or happy, smiling smirking vagrants, and out-at-elbows fellow-passengers and guests, with jests and quips and cranks, and hanky-panky even. On high roads and in inns, and alehouses, with travelling players, rogues and tramps, Dickens was quite at home; and what is yet more, he made us all quite at home with them: and he did it as Chaucer did it by thorough good spirits and "hail-fellow-well-met." And, with all his faults, he has this merit as well as some others, that he went willingly on pilgrimage always, and took others, promoting always love of comrades, fun, and humorous by-play. The latest great romancer, too, took his side: like Dickens, he was here full brother of Dan Chaucer, and followed him. How characteristic it is when he tells Mr Trigg that he preferred Samoa to Honolulu because it was more savage, and therefore yielded more *fun*.

CHAPTER XXX – LORD ROSEBERY'S CASE

Immediately on reading Lord Rosebery's address as Chairman of the meeting in Edinburgh to promote the erection of a monument to R. L. Stevenson, I wrote to him politely asking him whether, since he quoted a passage from a somewhat early essay by Stevenson naming the authors who had chiefly influenced him in point of style, his Lordship should not, merely in justice and for the sake of balance, have referred to Thoreau. I also remarked that Stevenson's later style sometimes showed too much self-conscious conflict of his various models in his mind while he was in the act of writing, and that this now and then imparted too much an air of artifice to his later compositions, and that those who knew most would be most troubled by it. Of that letter, I much regret now that I did not keep any copy; but I think I did incidentally refer to the friendship with which Stevenson had for so many years honoured me. This is a copy of the letter received in reply:

> "38 Berkeley Square, W.,
> 17*thDecember* 1896.
>
> "Dear Sir,—I am much obliged for your letter, and can only state that the name of Thoreau was not mentioned by Stevenson himself, and therefore I could not cite it in my quotation.
>
> "With regard to the style of Stevenson's later works, I am inclined to agree with you.-Believe me, yours very faithfully,
>
> Rosebery.
>
> "Dr Alexander H. Japp."

This I at once replied to as follows:

> "National Liberal Club,
> Whitehall Place, S.W.,
> 19*thDecember* 1896.
>
> "My Lord,—It is true R. L. Stevenson did not refer to Thoreau in the passage to which you allude,

for the good reason that he could not, since he did not know Thoreau till after it was written; but if you will oblige me and be so good as to turn to p. xix. of Preface, *By Way of Criticism*, to *Familiar Studies of Men and Books* you will read:

"'Upon me this pure, narrow, sunnily-ascetic Thoreau had exercised a wondrous charm. *I have scarce written ten sentences since I was introduced to him, but his influence might be somewhere detected by a close observer.*'

"It is very detectable in many passages of nature-description and of reflection. I write, my Lord, merely that, in case opportunity should arise, you might notice this fact. I am sure R. L. Stevenson would have liked it recognised.—I remain, my Lord, always yours faithfully, etc.,

Alexander H. Japp."

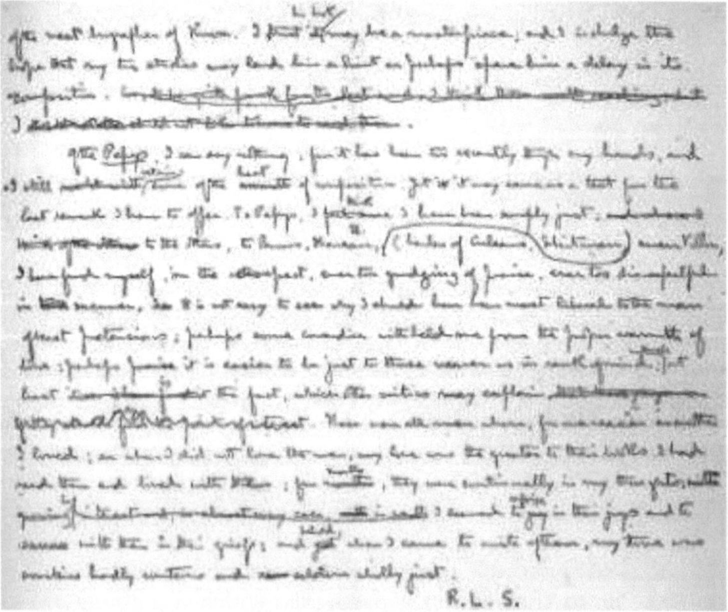
R. L. S.

In reply to this Lord Rosebery sent me only the most formal acknowledgment, not in the least encouraging me in any way to further aid him in the matter with regard to suggestions of any kind; so that I was helpless to press on his lordship the need for some corrections on other points which I would most willingly have tendered to him had he shown himself inclined or ready to receive them.

I might also have referred Lord Rosebery to the article in *The British Weekly* (*1887*), "Books that have Influenced Me," where, after having spoken of Shakespeare, the *Vicomte de Bragelonne*, Bunyan, Montaigne, Goethe, Martial, Marcus Aurelius's *Meditations*, and Wordsworth, he proceeds:

> "I suppose, when I am done, I shall find that I have forgotten much that is influential, as I see already I have forgotten Thoreau."

I need but to add to what has been said already that, had Lord Rosebery written and told me the result of his references and encouraged me to such an exercise, I should by-and-by have been very pleased to point out to him that he blundered, proving himself no master in Burns' literature, precisely as Mr Henley blundered about Burns' ancestry, when he gives confirmation to the idea that Burns came of a race of peasants on both sides, and was himself nothing but a peasant.

When the opportunity came to correct such blunders, corrections which I had even implored him to make, Lord Rosebery (who by several London papers had been spoken of as "knowing more than all the experts about all his themes"), that is, when his volume was being prepared for press, did not act on my good advice given him "*free, gratis, for nothing*"; no; he contented himself with simply slicing out columns from the *Times*, or allowing another man to do so for him, and reprinting them *literatim et verbatim*, all imperfect and misleading, as they stood. *Scripta manet* alas! only too truly exemplified to his disadvantage. But with that note of mine in his hand, protesting against an ominous and fatal omission as regards the confessed influences that had operated on Stevenson, he goes on, or allows Mr Geake to go on, quite as though he had verified matters and found that I was wrong as regards the facts on which I based my appeal to him for recognition of Thoreau as having influenced

Stevenson in style. Had he attended to correcting his serious errors about Stevenson, and some at least of those about Burns, thus adding, say, a dozen or twenty pages to his book wholly fresh and new and accurate, then the *Times* could not have got, even if it had sought, an injunction against his publishers and him; and there would have been no necessity that he should pad out other and later speeches by just a little whining over what was entirely due to his own disregard of good advice, his own neglect—his own fault—a neglect and a fault showing determination not to revise where revision in justice to his subject's own free and frank acknowledgments made it most essential and necessary.

Mr Justice North gave his decision against Lord Rosebery and his publishers, while the Lords of Appeal went in his favour; but the House of Lords reaffirmed the decision of Mr Justice North and granted a perpetual injunction against this book. The copyright in his speech is Lord Rosebery's, but the copyright in the *Times*' report is the *Times*'. You see one of the ideas underlying the law is that no manner of speech is quite perfect as the man speaks it, or is beyond revision, improvement, or extension, and, if there is but one *verbatim* report, as was the case of some of these speeches and addresses, then it is incumbent on the author, if he wishes to preserve his copyright, to revise and correct his speeches and addresses, so as to make them at least in details so far differ from the reported form. This thing ought Lord Rosebery to have done, on ethical and literary *grounds*, not to speak of legal and self-interested grounds; and I, for one, who from the first held exactly the view the House of Lords has affirmed, do confess that I have no sympathy for Lord Rosebery, since he had before him the suggestion and the materials for as substantial alterations and additions from my own hands, with as much more for other portions of his book, had he informed me of his appreciation, as would have saved him and his book from such a sadly ironical fate as has overtaken him and it.

From the whole business—since "free, gratis, for nothing," I offered him as good advice as any lawyer in the three kingdoms could have done for large payment, and since he never deemed it worth while, even to tell me the results of his reference to *Familiar Studies*, I here and now say deliberately that his conduct to me was scarcely so courteous and grateful and graceful as it might have been. How different—very different—the way in which the late R. L. Stevenson rewarded me for a literary service no whit greater or more essentially valuable to him than this service rendered to Lord Rosebery might have been to him.

This chapter would most probably not have been printed, had not Mr Coates re-issued the inadequate and most misleading paragraph about Mr Stevenson and style in his Lord Rosebery's *Life and Speeches* exactly as it was before, thus perpetuating at once the error and the wrong, in spite of all my trouble, warnings, and protests. It is a tragicomedy, if not a farce altogether, considering who are the principal actors in it. And let those who have copies of the queer prohibited book cherish them and thank me; for that I do by this give a new interest and value to it as a curiosity, law-inhibited, if not as high and conscientious literature—which it is not.

I remember very well about the time Lord Rosebery spoke on Burns, and Stevenson, and London, that certain London papers spoke of his deliverances as indicating more knowledge—fuller and exacter knowledge—of all these subjects than the greatest professed experts possessed. That is their extravagant and most reckless way, especially if the person spoken about is a "great politician" or a man of rank. They think they are safe with such superlatives applied to a brilliant and clever peer (with large estates and many interests), and an ex-Prime Minister! But literature is a republic, and it must here be said, though all unwillingly, that Lord Rosebery is but an amateur—a superficial though a clever amateur after all, and their extravagances do not change the fact. I declare him an amateur in Burns' literature and study because of what I have said elsewhere, and there are many points to add to that if need were. I have proved above from his own words that he was crassly and unpardonably ignorant of some of the most important points in R. L. Stevenson's development when he delivered that address in Edinburgh on Stevenson—a thing very, very pardonable—seeing that he is run after to do "speakings" of this sort; but to go on, in face of such warning and protest, printing his most misleading errors is not pardonable, and the legal recorded result is my justification and his condemnation, the more surely that even that would not awaken him so far as to cause him to restrain Mr Coates from reproducing in his *Life and Speeches*, just as it was originally, that peccant passage. I am fully ready to prove also that, though Chairman of the London County Council for a period, and though he made a very clever address at one of Sir W. Besant's lectures, there is much yet—very much—he might learn from Sir W. Besant's writings on London. It isn't so easy to outshine all the experts—even for a clever peer who has been Prime Minister, though it is very, very easy to flatter Lord Rosebery, with a purpose or purposes, as did at least once also with rarest tact, at Glasgow, indicating so many other things and possibilities, a certain very courtly ex-Moderator of the Church of Scotland.

CHAPTER XXXI – MR GOSSE AND MS. OF *TREASURE ISLAND*

Mr Edmund Gosse has been so good as to set down, with rather an air of too much authority, that both R. L. Stevenson and I deceived ourselves completely in the matter of my little share in the *Treasure Island* business, and that too much credit was sought by me or given to me, for the little service I rendered to R. L. Stevenson, and to the world, say, in helping to secure for it an element of pleasure through many generations. I have not *sought* any recognition from the world in this matter, and even the mention of it became so intolerable to me that I eschewed all writing about it, in the face of the most stupid and misleading statements, till Mr Sidney Colvin wrote and asked me to set down my account of the matter in my own words. This I did, as it would have been really rude to refuse a request so graciously made, and the reader has it in the *Academy* of 10th March 1900. Nevertheless, Mr Gosse's statements were revived and quoted, and the thing seemed ever to revolve again in a round of controversy.

Now, with regard to the reliability in this matter of Mr Edmund Gosse, let me copy here a little note made at request some time ago, dealing with two points. The first is this:

1. *Most assuredly* I carried away from Braemar in my portmanteau, as R. L. Stevenson says in *Idler's* article and in chapter of *My First Book* reprinted in *Edinburgh Edition*, several chapters of *Treasure Island*. On that point R. L. Stevenson, myself, and Mr James Henderson, to whom I took these, could not all be wrong and co-operating to mislead the public. These chapters, at least vii. or viii., as Mr Henderson remembers, would include the *first three*, that is, *finally revised versions for press*. Mr Gosse could not then *have heard R. L. Stevenson read from these final versions but from first draughts*only, and I am positively certain that with some of the later chapters R. L. Stevenson wrote them off-hand, and with great ease, and did not revise them to the extent of at all needing to re-write them, as I remember he was proud to tell me, being then fully in the vein, as he put it, and pleased to credit me with a share in this good result, and saying "my enthusiasm over it had set him up steep." There was

then, in my idea, a necessity that Stevenson should fill up a gap by verbal summary to Mr Gosse (which Mr Gosse has forgotten), bringing the incident up to a further point than Mr Gosse now thinks. I am certain of my facts under this head; and as Mr Gosse clearly fancies he heard R. L. Stevenson read all from final versions and is mistaken—*completely* mistaken there—he may be just as wrong and the victim of error or bad memory elsewhere after the lapse of more than twenty years.

2. I gave the pencilled outline of incident and plot to Mr Henderson—a fact he distinctly remembers. This fact completely meets and disposes of Mr Robert Leighton's quite imaginative *Billy Bo'sun* notion, and is absolute as to R. L. Stevenson before he left Braemar on the 21st September 1881, or even before I left it on 26th August 1881, having clear in his mind the whole scheme of the work, though we know very well that the absolute re-writing out finally for press of the concluding part of the book was done at Davos. Mr Henderson has always made it the strictest rule in his editorship that the complete outline of the plot and incident of the latter part of a story must be supplied to him, if the whole story is not submitted to him in MS.; and the agreement, if I am not much mistaken, was entered into days before R. L. Stevenson left Braemar, and when he came up to London some short time after to go to Weybridge, the only arrangement then needed to be made was about the forwarding of proofs to him.

The publication of *Treasure Island* in *Young Folks* began on the 1st October 1881, No. 565 and ran on in the following order:

October 1, 1881.
THE PROLOGUE

No. 565.
I. The Old Sea Dog at the Admiral Benbow.
II. Black Dog Appears and Disappears.

No. 566.
Dated *October* 8, 1881.
III. The Black Spot.

No. 567.
Dated *October* 15, 1881.

IV. The Sea Chart.
V. The Last of the Blind Man.
VI. The Captain's Papers.

No. 568.
Dated *October* 22, 1881.
THE STORY
I. I go to Bristol.
II. The Sea-Cook.
Ill. Powder and Arms.

Now, as the numbers of *Young Folks* were printed about a fortnight in advance of the date they bear under the title, it is clear that not only must the contract have been executed days before the middle of September, but that a large proportion of the *copy* must have been in Mr Henderson's hands at that date too, as he must have been entirely satisfied that the story would go on and be finished in a definite time. On no other terms would he have begun the publication of it. He was not in the least likely to have accepted a story from a man who, though known as an essayist, had not yet published anything in the way of a long story, on the ground merely of three chapters of prologue. Mr Gosse left Braemar on 5th September, when he says nine chapters were written, and Mr Henderson had offered terms for the story before the last of these could have reached him. That is on seeing, say six chapters of prologue. But when Mr Gosse speaks about three chapters only written, does he mean three of the prologue or three of the story, in addition to prologue, or what does he mean? The facts are clear. I took away in my portmanteau a large portion of the MS., together with a very full outline of the rest of the story, so that Mr Stevenson was, despite Mr Gosse's cavillings, *substantially* right when he wrote in *My First Book* in the *Idler*, etc., that "when he (Dr Japp) left us he carried away the manuscript in his portmanteau." There was nothing of the nature of an abandonment of the story at any point, nor any difficulty whatever arose in this respect in regard to it.

CHAPTER XXXII – STEVENSON PORTRAITS

Of the portraits of Stevenson a word or two may be said. There is a very good early photograph of him, taken not very long before the date of my visit to him at Braemar in 1881, and is an admirable likeness – characteristic not only in expression, but in pose and attitude, for it fixes him in a favourite position of his; and is, at the same time, very easy and natural. The velvet jacket, as I have remarked, was then his habitual wear, and the thin fingers holding the constant cigarette an inseparable associate and accompaniment.

He acknowledged himself that he was a difficult subject to paint – not at all a good sitter – impatient and apt to rebel at posing and time spent in arrangement of details – a fact he has himself, as we shall see, set on record in his funny verses to Count Nerli, who painted as successful a portrait as any. The little miniature, full-length, by Mr J. S. Sarjent, A.R.A., which was painted at Bournemouth in 1885, is confessedly a mere sketch and much of a caricature: it is in America. Sir W. B. Richmond has an unfinished portrait, painted in 1885 or 1886 – it has never passed out of the hands of the artist, – a photogravure from it is our frontispiece.

There is a medallion done by St Gauden's, representing Stevenson in bed propped up by pillows. It is thought to be a pretty good likeness, and it is now in Mr Sidney Colvin's possession. Others, drawings, etc., are not of much account.

And now we come to the Nerli portrait, of which so much has been written. Stevenson himself regarded it as the best portrait of him ever painted, and certainly it also is characteristic and effective, and though not what may be called a pleasant likeness, is probably a good representation of him in the later years of his life. Count Nerli actually undertook a voyage to Samoa in 1892, mainly with the idea of painting this portrait. He and Stevenson became great friends, as Stevenson naovely tells in the verses we have already referred to, but even this did not quite overcome Stevenson's restlessness. He avenged himself by composing these verses as he sat:

Did ever mortal man hear tell o' sic a ticklin' ferlie
As the comin' on to Apia here o' the painter Mr

Nerli?
He cam'; and, O, for o' human freen's o' a' he was the pearlie—
The pearl o' a' the painter folk was surely Mr Nerli.
He took a thraw to paint mysel'; he painted late and early;
O wow! the many a yawn I've yawned i' the beard o' Mr Nerli.
Whiles I wad sleep and whiles wad wake, an' whiles was mair than surly;
I wondered sair as I sat there fornent the eyes o' Nerli.
O will he paint me the way I want, as bonnie as a girlie?
O will he paint me an ugly tyke?—and be d-d to Mr Nerli.
But still an' on whichever it be, he is a canty kerlie,
The Lord protect the back an' neck o' honest Mr Nerli.

Mr Hammerton gives this account of the Nerli portrait:

> "The history of the Nerli portrait is peculiar. After being exhibited for some time in New Zealand it was bought, in the course of this year, by a lady who was travelling there, for a hundred guineas. She then offered it for that sum to the Scottish National Portrait Gallery; but the Trustees of the Board of Manufactures—that oddly named body to which is entrusted the fostering care of Art in Scotland, and, in consequence, the superintendence of the National Portrait Gallery—did not see their way to accept the offer. Some surprise has been expressed at the action of the Trustees in thus declining to avail themselves of the opportunity of obtaining the portrait of one of the most distinguished Scotsmen of recent times. It can hardly have been for want of money, for though the funds at their disposal for the purchase of ordinary

works of art are but limited, no longer ago than last year they were the recipients of a very handsome legacy from the late Mr J. M. Gray, the accomplished and much lamented Curator of the Scottish National Portrait Gallery—a legacy left them for the express purpose of acquiring portraits of distinguished Scotsmen, and the income of which was amply sufficient to have enabled them to purchase this portrait. One is therefore almost shut up to the conclusion that the Trustees were influenced in their decision by one of the two following reasons:

"1. That they did not consider Stevenson worthy of a place in the gallery. This is a position so incomprehensible and so utterly opposed to public sentiment that one can hardly credit it having been the cause of this refusal. Whatever may be the place which Stevenson may ultimately take as an author, and however opinions may differ as to the merits of his work, no one can deny that he was one of the most popular writers of his day, and that as a mere master of style, if for nothing else, his works will be read so long as there are students of English Literature. Surely the portrait of one for whom such a claim may legitimately be made cannot be considered altogether unworthy of a place in the National Collection, as one of Scotland's most distinguished sons.

"2. The only other reason which can be suggested as having weighed with the Trustees in their decision is one which in some cases might be held to be worthy of consideration. It is conceivable that in the case of some men the Trustees might be of opinion that there was plenty of time to consider the matter, and that in the meantime there was always the chance of some generous donor presenting them with a portrait. But, as has been shown above, the portraits of Stevenson are practically confined to two: one of these is in America, and there is not the least chance of its ever coming here; and the other they have refused. And, as it is understood that the Trustees have a rule that they do not accept any portrait which has not been painted from the life, they preclude themselves from acquiring a copy of any existing picture or even a portrait done from memory.

"It is rumoured that the Nerli portrait may ultimately find a resting-place in the National Collection of Portraits in London. If this should prove to be the case, what a commentary on the old saying: 'A prophet is not without honour save in his own country.'"

CHAPTER XXXIII – LAPSES AND ERRORS IN CRITICISM

Nothing could perhaps be more wearisome than to travel o'er the wide sandy area of Stevenson criticism and commentary, and expose the many and sad and grotesque errors that meet one there. Mr Baildon's slip is innocent, compared with many when he says (p. 106) *Treasure Island* appeared in *Young Folks* as *The Sea-Cook*. It did nothing of the kind; it is on plain record in print, even in the pages of the *Edinburgh Edition*, that Mr James Henderson would not have the title *The Sea-Cook*, as he did not like it, and insisted on its being *Treasure Island*. To him, therefore, the vastly better title is due. Mr Henley was in doubt if Mr Henderson was still alive when he wrote the brilliant and elevated article on "Some Novels" in the *North American*, and as a certain dark bird killed Cock Robin, so he killed off Dr Japp, and not to be outdone, got in an ideal "Colonel" *Jack*; so Mr Baildon there follows Henley, unaware that Mr Henderson did not like *The Sea-Cook*, and was still alive, and that a certain Jack in the fatal *North American* has Japp's credit.

Mr Baildon's words are:

> "This was the famous book of adventure, *Treasure Island*, appearing first as *The Sea-Cook* in a boy's paper, where it made no great stir. But, on its publication in volume form, with the vastly better title, the book at once 'boomed,' as the phrase goes, to an extent then, in 1882, almost unprecedented. The secret of its immense success may almost be expressed in a phrase by saying that it is a book like *Gulliver's Travels*, *The Pilgrim's Progress*, and *Robinson Crusoe* itself for all ages – boys, men, and women."

Which just shows how far lapse as to a fact may lead to critical misreadings also.

Mr Hammerton sometimes lets good folks say in his pages, without correction, what is certainly not correct. Thus at one place we are told that Stevenson was only known as Louis in print, whereas that was the only name by which he was known in his own family. Then Mr Gosse, at p. 34, is allowed to write:

> "Professor Blackie was among them on the steamer from the Hebrides, a famous figure that calls for no description, and a voluble shaggy man, clad in homespun, with spectacles forward upon his nose, who it was whispered to us, was Mr Sam Bough, the Scottish Academician, *a water-colour painter of some repute*, who was to die in 1878."

Mr Sam Bough *was* "a water-colour painter of some repute," but a painter in oils of yet greater repute—a man of rare strength, resource, and facility—never, perhaps, wholly escaping from some traces of his early experiences in scene-painting, but a true genius in his art. Ah, well I remember him, though an older man, yet youthful in the band of young Scotch artists among whom as a youngster I was privileged to move in Edinburgh—Pettie, Chalmers, M'Whirter, Peter Graham, MacTaggart, MacDonald, John Burr, and Bough. Bough could be voluble on art; and many a talk I had with him as with the others named, especially with John Burr. Bough and he both could talk as well as paint, and talk right well. Bough had a slight cast in the eye; when he got a *wee* excited on his subject he would come close to you with head shaking, and spectacles displaced, and forelock wagging, and the cast would seem to die away. Was this a fact, or was it an illusion on my part? I have often asked myself that question, and now I ask it of others. Can any of my good friends in Edinburgh say; can Mr Caw help me here, either to confirm or to correct me? I venture to insert here an anecdote, with which my friend of old days, Mr Wm. MacTaggart, R.S.A., in a letter kindly favours me:

> "Sam Bough was a very sociable man; and, when on a sketching tour, liked to have a young artist or two with him. Jack Nisbett played the violin, and Sam the 'cello, etc. Jack was fond of telling that Sam used to let them all choose the best views, and then he would take what was left; and Jack, with mild astonishment, would say, that 'it generally turned out to be the best—on the canvas!'"

In Mr Hammerton's copy of the verses in reply to Mr Crockett's dedication of *The Stickit Minister* to Stevenson, in which occurred the fine phrase "The grey Galloway lands, where about the graves of the martyrs the whaups are crying, his heart remembers how":

"Blows the wind to-day and the sun and the rain
are flying:
Blows the wind on the moors to-day and now,
Where about the graves of the martyrs the whaups
are crying,
My heart remembers how.

"Grey recumbent tombs of the dead in desert
places,
Standing stones on the vacant wine-red moor,
Hills of sheep, and the *homes* of the silent vanished
races,
And winds austere and pure.

"Be it granted me to behold you again in dying,
Hills of home! and to hear again the call—
Hear about the graves of the martyrs the pee-weet
crying,
And hear no more at all."

Mr Hammerton prints *howes* instead of *homes*, which I have italicised above. And I may note, though it does not affect the poetry, if it does a little affect the natural history, that the *pee-weets* and the whaups are not the same—the one is the curlew, and the other is the lapwing—the one most frequenting wild, heathery or peaty moorland, and the other pasture or even ploughed land—so that it is a great pity for unity and simplicity alike that Stevenson did not repeat the "whaup," but wrote rather as though pee-weet or pee-weets were the same as whaups—the common call of the one is *Ker-lee, ker-lee,* and of the other *pee-weet, pee-weet,* hence its common name.

It is a pity, too, that Mr Hammerton has no records of some portions of the life at Davos Platz. Not only was Stevenson ill there in April 1892, but his wife collapsed, and the tender concern for her made havoc with some details of his literary work. It is good to know this. Such errata or omissions throw a finer light on his character than controlling perfection would do. Ah, I remember how my old friend W. B. Rands ("Matthew Browne" and "Henry Holbeach") was wont to declare that were men perfect they would be isolated, if not idiotic, that we are united to each other by our defects—that even physical beauty would be dead like later Greek statues, were these not departures from the perfect lines. The letter given by me at p. 28 transfigures in its light, some of his work at that time.

And then what an opportunity, we deeply regret to say, Mr Hammerton wholly missed, when he passed over without due explanation or commentary that most significant pamphlet—the *Address to the Scottish Clergy*. If Mr Hammerton had but duly and closely studied that and its bearings and suggestions in many directions, then he would have written such a chapter for true enlightenment and for interest as exactly his book—attractive though it is in much—yet specially lacks. It is to be hoped that Mr Sidney Colvin will not once more miss the chance which is thus still left open to him to perfect his *Life of Stevenson*, and make it more interpretive than anything yet published. If he does this, then, a dreadful *lacuna* in the *Edinburgh Edition* will also be supplied.

Carefully reading over again Mr Arthur Symons' *Studies in Two Literatures*—published some years ago—I have come across instances of apparent contradiction which, so far as I can see, he does not critically altogether reconcile, despite his ingenuity and great charm of style. One relates to Thoreau, who, while still "sturdy" as Emerson says, "and like an elm tree," as his sister Sophia says, showed exactly the same love of nature and power of interpreting her as he did after in his later comparatively short period of "invalidity," while Mr Symons says his view of Nature absolutely was that of the invalid, classing him unqualifiedly with Jefferies and Stevenson, as invalid. Thoreau's mark even in the short later period of "invalidity" was complete and robust independence and triumph over it—a thing which I have no doubt wholly captivated Stevenson, as scarce anything else would have done, as a victory in the exact *rtle* he himself was most ambitious to fill. For did not he too wrestle well with the "wolverine" he carried on his back—in this like Addington Symonds and Alexander Pope? Surely I cannot be wrong here to reinforce my statement by a passage from a letter written by Sophia Thoreau to her good friend Daniel Ricketson, after her brother's death, the more that R. L. Stevenson would have greatly exulted too in its cheery and invincible stoicism:

> "Profound joy mingles with my grief. I feel as if something very beautiful had happened—not death; although Henry is with us no longer, yet the memory of his sweet and virtuous soul must ever cheer and comfort me. My heart is filled with praise to God for the gift of such a brother, and may I never distrust the love and wisdom of Him who made him and who has now called him to labour in more glorious fields than earth affords. You ask for some particulars relating to Henry's illness. I feel like saying that Henry was never affected, never reached by it. I never before saw such a manifestation of the power of spirit over matter. Very often I heard him tell his visitors that he enjoyed existence as well as ever. The thought of death, he said, did not trouble him. His thoughts had entertained him all his life and did still. . . . He considered occupation as necessary for the sick as for those in health, and accomplished a vast amount of labour in those last few months."

A rare "invalidity" this—a little confusing easy classifications. I think Stevenson would have felt and said that brother and sister were well worthy of each other; and that the sister was almost as grand and cheery a stoic, with no literary profession of it, as was the brother.

The other thing relates to Stevenson's *human soul.* I find Mr Symons says, at p. 243, that Stevenson "had something a trifle elfish and uncanny about him, as of a bewitched being who was not actually human—had not actually a human soul"—in which there may be a glimmer of truth viewed from his revelation of artistic curiosities in some aspects, but is hardly true of him otherwise; and this Mr Symons himself seems to have felt, when, at p. 246, he writes: "He is one of those writers who speak *to us on easy terms,* with whom we *may exchange affections.*" How "affections" could be exchanged on easy terms between the normal human being and an elfish creature actually *without a human soul* (seeing that affections are, as Mr Matthew Arnold might have said, at least, three-fourths of soul) is more, I confess, than I can quite see at present; but in this rather *maladroit* contradiction Mr Symons does point at one phase of the problem of Stevenson—this, namely that to all the ordinary happy or pleasure-endings he opposes, as it were of set purpose, gloom, as though to certain things he was quite indifferent, and though, as we have seen, his actual life and practice were quite opposed to this.

I am sorry I *cannot* find the link in Mr Symons' essay, which would quite make these two statements consistently coincide critically. As an enthusiastic, though I hope still a discriminating, Stevensonian, I do wish Mr Symons would help us to it somehow hereafter. It would be well worth his doing, in my opinion.

CHAPTER XXXIV – LETTERS AND POEMS IN TESTIMONY

Among many letters received by me in acknowledgment of, or in commentary on, my little tributes to R. L. Stevenson, in various journals and magazines, I find the following, which I give here for reasons purely personal, and because my readers may with me, join in admiration of the fancy, grace and beauty of the poems. I must preface the first poem by a letter, which explains the genesis of the poem, and relates a striking and very touching incident:

> "37 St Donatt's Road,
> Lewisham High Road, S.E.,
> 1st*March* 1895.
>
> "Dear Sir, – As you have written so much about your friend, the late Robert Louis Stevenson, and quoted many tributes to his genius from contemporary writers, I take the liberty of sending you herewith some verses of mine which appeared in *The Weekly Sun* of November last. I sent a copy of these verses to Samoa, but unfortunately the great novelist died before they reached it. I have, however, this week, received a little note from Mrs Strong, which runs as follows:
>
> "'Your poem of "Greeting" came too late. I can only thank you by sending a little moss that I plucked from a tree overhanging his grave on Vaea Mountain.'
>
> "I trust you will appreciate my motive in sending you the poem. I do not wish to obtrude my claims as a verse-writer upon your notice, but I thought the incident I have recited would be interesting to one who is so devoted a collector of Stevensoniana. – Respectfully yours,
>
> F. J. Cox."

GREETING

(TO ROBERT LOUIS STEVENSON, IN SAMOA)

We, pent in cities, prisoned in the mart,
Can know you only as a man apart,
But ever-present through your matchless art.

You have exchanged the old, familiar ways
For isles, where, through the range of splendid days,
Her treasure Nature lavishly displays.

There, by the gracious sweep of ampler seas,
That swell responsive to the odorous breeze.
You have the wine of Life, and we the lees!

You mark, perchance, within your island bowers,
The slow departure of the languorous hours,
And breathe the sweetness of the strange wild-flowers.

And everything your soul and sense delights—
But in the solemn wonder of your nights,
When Peace her message on the landscape writes;

When Ocean scarcely flecks her marge with foam—
Your thoughts must sometimes from your island roam,
To centre on the sober face of Home.

Though many a league of water rolls between
The simple beauty of an English scene,
From all these wilder charms your love may wean.

Some kindly sprite may bring you as a boon
Sweets from the rose that crowns imperial June,
Or reminiscence of the throstle's tune;

Yea, gladly grant you, with a generous hand,
Far glimpses of the winding, wind-swept strand,
The glens and mountains of your native land,

Until you hear the pipes upon the breeze—
But wake unto the wild realities
The tangled forests and the boundless seas!

For lo! the moonless night has passed away,
A sudden dawn dispels the shadows grey,
The glad sea moves and hails the quickening day.

New life within the arbours of your fief
Awakes the blossom, quivers in the leaf,
And splendour flames upon the coral reef.

If such a prospect stimulate your art,
More than our meadows where the shadows dart,
More than the life which throbs in London's heart,

Then stay, encircled by your Southern bowers,
And weave, amid the incense of the flowers,
The skein of fair romance—the gain is ours!

F. J. Cox.

Weekly Sun, 11*th* November 1904.

R. L. S., IN MEMORIAM.

An elfin wight as e'er from faeryland
Came to us straight with favour in his eyes,
Of wondrous seed that led him to the prize
Of fancy, with the magic rod in hand.
Ah, there in faeryland we saw him stand,
As for a while he walked with smiles and sighs,
Amongst us, finding still the gem that buys
Delight and joy at genius's command.

And now thy place is empty: fare thee well;
Thou livest still in hearts that owe thee more
Than gold can reckon; for thy richer store
Is of the good that with us aye most dwell.
Farewell; sleep sound on Vaea's windy shrine,
While round the songsters join their song to thine.

A. C. R.

APPENDIX

The following appeared some time ago in one of the London evening papers, and I make bold, because of its truth and vigour, to insert it here:

THE LAND OF STEVENSON, *ON AN AFTERNOON'S WALK*

Will there be a "Land of Stevenson," as there is already a "Land of Burns," or a "Land of Scott," known to the tourist, bescribbled by the guide-book maker? This the future must tell. Yet will it be easy to mark out the bounds of "Robert Louis Stevenson's Country"; and, taking his native and well-loved city for a starting-point, a stout walker may visit all its principal sites in an afternoon. The house where he was born is within a bowshot of the Water of Leith; some five miles to the south are Caerketton and Allermuir, and other crests of the Pentlands, and below them Swanston Farm, where year after year, in his father's time, he spent the summer days basking on the hill slopes; two or three miles to the westward of Swanston is Colinton, where his mother's father, Dr Balfour, was minister; and here again you are back to the Water of Leith, which you can follow down to the New Town. In this triangular space Stevenson's memories and affections were firmly rooted; the fibres could not be withdrawn from the soil, and "the voice of the blood" and the longing for this little piece of earth make themselves plaintively heard in his last notes. By Lothian Road, after which Stevenson quaintly thought of naming the new edition of his works, and past Boroughmuirhead and the "Bore Stane," where James FitzJames set up his standard before Flodden, wends your southward way to the hills. The builder of suburban villas has pushed his handiwork far into the fields since Stevenson was wont to tramp between thc city and the Pentlands; and you may look in vain for the flat stone whereon, as the marvelling child was told, there once rose a "crow-haunted gibbet." Three-quarters of an hour of easy walking, after you have cleared the last of the houses will bring you to Swanston; and half an hour more will take the stiff climber, a little breathless, to

THE TOP OF CAERKETTON CRAGS.

You may follow the high road—indeed there is a choice of two, drawn at different levels—athwart the western skirts of the Braid Hills, now tenanted, crown and sides of them, by golf; then to the crossroads of Fairmilehead, whence the road dips down, to rise again and circumvent the most easterly wing of the Pentlands. You would like to pursue this route, were it only to look down on Bow Bridge and recall how the last-century gauger used to put together his flute and play "Over the hills and far away" as a signal to his friend in the distillery below, now converted into a dairy farm, to stow away his barrels. Better it is, however, to climb the stile just past the poor-house gate, and follow the footpath along the smoothly scooped banks of the Braid Burn to "Cockmylane" and to Comiston. The wind has been busy all the morning spreading the snow over a glittering world. The drifts are piled shoulder-high in the lane as it approaches Comiston, and each old tree grouped around the historic mansion is outlined in snow so virgin pure that were the Ghost—"a lady in white, with the most beautiful clear shoes on her feet"—to step out through the back gate, she would be invisible, unless, indeed, she were between you and the ivy-draped dovecot wall. Near by, at the corner of the Dreghorn Woods, is the Hunters' Tryst, on the roof of which, when it was still a wayside inn, the Devil was wont to dance on windy nights. In the field through which you trudge knee-deep in drift rises the "Kay Stane," looking to-day like a tall monolith of whitest marble. Stevenson was mistaken when he said that it was from its top a neighbouring laird, on pain of losing his lands, had to "wind a blast of bugle horn" each time the King

VISITED HIS FOREST OF PENTLAND.

That honour belongs to another on the adjacent farm of Buckstane. The ancient monument carries you further back, and there are Celtic authorities that translate its name the "Stone of Victory." The "Pechtland Hills"—their elder name—were once a refuge for the Picts; and Caerketton—probably Caer-etin, the giant's stronghold—is one of them. Darkly its cliffs frown down upon you, while all else is flashing white in the winter sunlight. For once, in this last buttress thrown out into the plain of Lothian towards the royal city, the outer folds of the Pentlands loses its boldly-rounded curves, and drops an almost sheer descent of black rock to the little glen below. In a wrinkle of the foothills Swanston farm and hamlet are snugly tucked away. The spirit that breathes about it in summer time is gently pastoral. It is sheltered from the rougher blasts; it is set about with trees and green hills. It was with this aspect of the place that Stevenson, coming hither on holiday, was best acquainted. The village green, whereon the windows of the neat white cottages turn a kindly gaze under low brows of thatch, is then a perfect place in which to rest, and, watching the smoke rising and listening to "the leaves ruffling in the breeze," to muse on men and things; especially on Sabbath mornings, when the ploughman or shepherd, "perplext wi' leisure," it is time to set forth on the three-mile walk along the hill-skirts to Colinton kirk. But Swanston in winter time must also

HAVE BEEN FAMILIAR TO STEVENSON.

Snow-wreathed Pentlands, the ribbed and furrowed front of Cae-rketton, the low sun striking athwart the sloping fields of white, the shadows creeping out from the hills, and the frosty yellow fog dra-wing in from the Firth—must often have flashed back on the thoug-hts of the exile of Samoa. Against this wintry background the white farmhouse, old and crow-stepped, looks dingy enough; the garden is heaped with the fantastic treasures of the snow; and when you toil heavily up the waterside to the clump of pines and beeches you find yourself in a fairy forest. One need not search to-day for the pool where the lynx-eyed John Todd, "the oldest herd on the Pent-lands," watched from behind the low scrag of wood the stranger collie come furtively to wash away the tell-tale stains of lamb's blood. The effacing hand of the snow has smothered it over. Higher you mount, mid leg-deep in drift, up the steep and slippery hill-face, to the summit. Edinburgh has been creeping nearer since Ste-venson's musing fancy began to draw on the memories of the climbs up "steep Caerketton." But this light gives it a mystic dis-tance; and it is all glitter and shadow. Arthur Seat is like some great sea monster stranded near a city of dreams; from the fog-swathed Firth gleams the white walls of Inchkeith lighthouse, a mark never missed by Stevenson's father's son; above Fife rise the twin breasts of the Lomonds. Or turn round and look across the Esk valley to the

Moorfoots; or more westerly, where the back range of the Pentlands—Caernethy, the Scald, and the knife-edged Kips—draw a sharp silhouette of Arctic peaks against the sky. In the cloven hollow between is Glencarse Loch, an ancient chapel and burying ground hidden under its waters; on the slope above it, not a couple miles away, is Rullion Green, where, as Stevenson told in *The Pentland Rising* (his first printed work)

THE WESTLAND WHIGS WERE SCATTERED

as chaff on the hills. Were "topmost Allermuir," that rises close beside you, removed from his place, we might see the gap in the range through which Tom Dalyell and his troopers spurred from Currie to the fray. The air on these heights is invigorating as wine; but it is also keen as a razor. Without delaying long yon plunge down to the "Windy Door Nick"; follow the "nameless trickle that springs from the green bosom of Allermuir," past the rock and pool, where, on summer evenings, the poet "loved to sit and make bad verses"; and cross Halkerside and the Shearers' Knowe, those "adjacent cantons on a single shoulder of a hill," sometimes floundering to the neck in the loose snow of a drain, sometimes scaring the sheep huddling in the wreaths, or putting up a covey of moorfowl that circle back without a cry to cover in the ling. In an hour you are at Colinton, whose dell has on one side the manse garden, where a bright-eyed boy, who was to become famous, spent so much of his time when he came thither on visits to his stern Presbyterian grandfather; on the other the old churchyard. The snow has drawn its cloak of ermine over the sleepers, it has run its fingers over the worn lettering; and records almost effaced start out from the stone. In vain these "voices of generations dead" summon their wandering child, though you might deem that his spirit would rest more quietly where the cold breeze from Pentland shakes the ghostly trees in Colinton Dell than "under the flailing fans and shadows of the palm."

Footnotes:

[1] Professor Charles Warren Stoddard, Professor of English Literature at the Catholic University of Washington, in *Kate Field's Washington.*

[2] In his portrait-sketch of his father, Stevenson speaks of him as a "man of somewhat antique strain, and with a blended sternness and softness that was wholly Scottish, and at first sight somewhat bewildering," as melancholy, and with a keen sense of his unworthiness, yet humorous in company; shrewd and childish; a capital adviser.

[3] *Inferno,* Canto XV.

[4] Alas, I never was told that remark—when I saw my friend afterwards there was always too much to talk of else, and I forgot to ask.

[5] Quoted by Hammerton, pp. 2 and 3.

[6] Tusitala, as the reader must know, is the Samoan for Teller of Tales.

[7] *Wisdom of Goethe,* p. 38.

[8] *The Foreigner at Home,* in *Memories and Portraits.*

[9] A great deal has been made of the "John Bull element" in De Quincey since his *Memoir* was written by me (see *Masson's Condensation,* p. 95); so now perhaps a little more may be made of the rather conceited Calvinistic Scot element in R. L. Stevenson!

[10] It was Mr George Moore who said this.

[11] *Fortnightly Review,* October, 1903.